IMMORTAL IMAGES

July 29, 1999

To Ashley —
Thanks so much for all of your help, and best of luck in all of your future endeavors

From Jim
Kristy ☺
Sam Ammy ♡

IMMORTAL IMAGES

The Jade Collection of Margaret and Trammell Crow

by
Alex Kerr

curator
Larry Niblett

Published by Crow Family Interests
© Crow Family Interests, Dallas, 1989

All rights reserved. No part of this publication may be reproduced, stored in a retrieval system, or transmitted in any form or by any means, electronic, mechanical, photocopying, recording or otherwise, without prior permission of the Publishers.

ISBN 0-9622743-0-5

Project Coordinated by Lucilo A. Peña

Design and Production Art by Tom Dawson and Bill Maize, DUO design group, Fort Worth

Photography by Lydia Cutter and Tricia Smith, Cutter/Smith Photographics, Dallas © 1989

Separations by JTM Colorscan, Inc., Fort Worth

Printed by Hurst Printing Company, Dallas

Typeset by LinoTypographers, Inc., Fort Worth

Preceding page:
Bi disk, Song, 11th–13th century, 8 in. diam. (detail)

Frontispiece:
Water buffalo, dark green jade, Qing, early 18th century, W 18.25 in.

To Mom and Dad

From

Bob, Howard, Harlan,
Trammell, Lucy, and Stuart

Contents

Chronology X
Acknowledgments XI
The Collection 1-3
History of Jade 4-7
Archaic and Archaism 8-15
Natural Boulders and Pebbles 16-21
Plants 22-23
Government and Ritual 24-29
Incense 30-35
Animals and Birds 36-43
Mythical Animals 44-47
The Human Figure 48-51
Courtly Life 52-60
Vessels 61-67
The Scholar 68-73
Table Screens 74-81
Small Pieces 82-87
Sino-Tibetan 88-89
Inset Screens and Panels 90-93
The Moghul Style 94-99
Jewelry 100-103
Bibliography and Index 106-109

Opposite page:
Table screen, green nephrite, Qing, Qianlong period [1736-1795], H 26 in. W 19 in. (detail)

Chronology

Dynasties:

Neolithic Period	8000 BC-1765 BC
Shang	1766 BC-1122 BC
Western Zhou	1122 BC-722 BC
Eastern Zhou	722 BC-221 BC
Spring and Autumn Period	722 BC-481 BC
Warring States Period	481 BC-221 BC
Former Han	206 BC-9 AD
Later Han	25-220
Early Medieval Period	221-618
Tang	618-907
Song	960-1279
Yuan	1280-1368
Ming	1368-1644
Qing	1644-1912

Reign Periods:

Shun Zhi	1644-1661
Kang Xi	1662-1722
Yong Zheng	1723-1736
Qianlong	1736-1795
Guang Xu	1875-1908

Acknowledgments

"When a gentleman reads this book and is able to discern the difference between jade and stone, he will likewise learn to distinguish the jade and stone among men," wrote a Ming collector. But distinguishing between jade and stone is not an easy task.

The field of jade covers many different disciplines: from art history to chemistry. In particular, the dating of jade is notoriously difficult. This book would not have been possible without kind offerings of advice and expertise from scholars and collectors. Our sincere thanks to:

Michael Aris, Research Fellow in Himalayan and Tibetan Studies, Wolfson College, Oxford

Robert Hatfield Ellsworth, New York

Irene Martin, Administrative Director and Curator of the Thyssen-Bornemisza Foundation, Lugano, Switzerland

Robert Mowry, Assistant Curator of Asian Art, Sackler Museum, Harvard University

John Rosenfield, Curator of Asian Art, Sackler Museum, Harvard University

Emily Sano, Formerly Curator of Asian Art, Kimbell Museum; now Deputy Director of the Dallas Museum of Art

Lawrence Wu, New York

Also, many thanks to those who gave their time to help with the production of the book: William Gilkey, Bobbye Johnson, Jim Kelley, Linda Middleton, Mark Nathanson, Toshihiro Otani, Dui Seid, Hideo Shimada, Southern Methodist University Publications, Lauren Vastine, and Rodney Yoder.

NATIONAL PALACE MUSEUM
SHIH-LIN, TAIPEI 111
TAIWAN
REPUBLIC OF CHINA

OFFICE OF THE DIRECTOR

March 27, 1989

China is the world's longest unbroken cultural tradition, and from the earliest years, jade has played a pivotal role. The ancient sages held jade to be symbolic of the highest human virtues, and for this reason jade implements were used in religious rituals and as the insignia of kingship.

In later dynasties, jade developed as an art form. The art of jade carving touches on all aspects of the Chinese ideals: respect for natural forms, elegant shape, technical excellence, literary and philosophical nuance. He who loves jade, loves China.

Mr. Trammell Crow has amassed one of the finest collections of jade in private hands in the world today. The collection specializes in later periods, in particular Late Ming and Ch'ien Lung jades, from a time when jade carving reached its highest peak of refinement.

The Trammell Crow collection is significant because of its wide scope—covering everything from Imperial seals to hairpins. From this collection we can learn much concerning the marvelous material that is jade, and much concerning the Chinese view of the world. It is my hope that this first publication of Mr. Trammel Crow's collection will spur greater appreciation for the arts and history of China.

Chin Hsiao-yi
Director
National Palace Museum, Taipei
Republic of China

Opposite page:
Carved boulder, Qing, Qianlong period [1736–1795], H 19 in. (detail)

History of Jade

A love of jade links the modern world to the Stone Age. It is the only material which has been continuously valued, predating by thousands of years the appearance of bronze and iron. Those materials, once precious, are commonplace today, but jade is still treasured, the finest jade of more value than gold and diamonds.

Nephrite and Jadeite

In ancient times, the Chinese called many different minerals "jade," the word meaning any hard and beautiful stone. Today jade is limited to only two minerals: nephrite and jadeite.

Nephrite is the "classical" stone, the jade used in ancient ritual and comprising for most Chinese jade carvings until the 18th century. Nephrite traditionally came from the neighborhood of Khotan in western China, where boulders of jade were collected in the riverbeds.

Near the end of the 18th century, the Chinese discovered another material, mined in Burma. This was jadeite, similar to nephrite, but harder and more brilliant in color.

Nephrite and jadeite have different chemical structures. Nephrite is a silicate of calcium and magnesium, with a hardness of 6.5 on Mohs' scale (talc is 1, diamond is 10). It has a fibrous structure so dense that it cannot be seen except under a powerful microscope. This makes it one of the toughest of all stones. In one test it took fifty tons of pressure to crush a cubic inch. The dense structure gives nephrite an oily or soapy surface texture.

Jadeite is a silicate of sodium and aluminum, 6.75-7 on Mohs' scale of hardness. While harder than nephrite, it will show crystalline fibers if held up to light and is somewhat more brittle. Jadeite takes a glassy finish in contrast to the more subdued texture of nephrite. The finest jadeite, of pure jewel-like color, is ranked with emeralds and rubies.

Today, jadeite has overtaken nephrite as the stone of modern carving because of its brilliant colors. But nephrite is still valued as the "serious" stone, the jade that the ancients thought divine.

Hardness and Color

Jade cannot be "carved" since it is harder than most chisels. It is ground and polished with drills, using sand or other abrasives mixed with water. The old grinding process, using a foot treadle to turn the drill, was extremely laborious, one piece taking

Spider and two crickets on a leaf, jadeite, late Qing, ca. 1900. W 9.37 in.

The carver has used the russet skin of the jade boulder for the leaf, bringing out the bright jadeite greens in the three insects.

Yellow-green nephrite

The collection is scattered across the country, in the hands of different owners. Bringing all these pieces together for photography and research, and at the same time keeping the book a surprise for Trammell's and Margaret's birthdays, was a task to baffle the most artful Chinese sage.

Choosing the 130 objects illustrated in this book involved many heartbreaking decisions. For every piece illustrated, others equally beautiful and important are not shown. We have attempted to give a sense of the scope of the collection, and to demonstrate the way it reflects so many aspects of Chinese culture: from archaic ritual, through the world of the scholars, to the refinements of courtly life.

Jade in its many manifestations symbolizes China, and Trammell Crow's true love is China and the Far East. "I cannot say why it is," he says, pointing to his heart, "But these objects *move* me." He and Margaret have taken numerous trips to China, as well as other Asian nations, from India to Japan. Their interest is by no means limited to the past. The Trammell Crow Company is today very active in Japan and China. "Asia is the future," he says.

Jade is a mysterious material, thought by the Chinese to symbolize the human virtues. "I have always believed that knowledge of these artifacts helps you with a knowledge of people," Trammell Crow has said. For those who have seen these pieces on site in the offices in Dallas, this book will illustrate the world of China from which they came. For those who love the East, the jade will provide an insight into the ideals and values of Asia.

Asian artworks awaiting placement in Dallas

The Collection

"I have no expensive vices," Trammell Crow announces to the visitor with customary directness. "I don't smoke and I don't drink. I'm devoted to my wife and I'm strict with my children. But I do have one passion—and it is these Chinese things!" And he points towards a shelf of jades and spirit stones. And with this, he initiates another friend to the collection.

The collection is everywhere, a constant presence wherever Trammell Crow companies are active in Dallas. Step out of the elevator at the 35th floor headquarters of the Trammell Crow Company: to the right stands a carved jade boulder, and to the left a tall porcelain Guanyin. Executives in the investment section face a set of four luminous jade screens. Downstairs, on the 32nd floor, an accountant in the international section looks up from his financial calculations to see a huge bronze Tibetan magical dagger.

Over at the Market Center offices, Japanese screens line the walls in all directions. Meanwhile, in the lobby of the Anatole hotel, guests enter the elevators by a shelf of Qianlong jades. But perhaps because the collection is everywhere so evident, very few people have a sense of its true extent.

It began with a single piece of jade purchased in 1971. By 1974 Trammell Crow had taken the step of purchasing an entire collection: the Moss collection of over 140 pieces.

Jade cabinet in the Crow's residence

Opposite page: Margaret and Trammell Crow (*Photo: Randall Hahn*)

Huang Guo Shu waterfall, Guizhou Province, Crow trip to South China, May 1988. (*Photo: Don Madsen*)

Today, the jade collection amounts to over 1,200 pieces, plus dozens of hardstone carvings in other materials: carnelian, malachite, chalcedony, lapis, goldstone, turquoise, jasper, rock crystal, etc.

From jades and hardstones, he moved on to other types of Asian art, encompassing Indian, Khmer, Burmese, Thai, Nepalese, and Tibetan statuary, Persian rugs, Chinese Tang porcelains, and Japanese screens and bronzes. From Asian art he expanded to Western art, with holdings covering many areas, from early German painting to contemporary East European sculpture.

The strength of the collection is sculpture and architectural pieces, some on a massive scale. Trammell Crow has not hesitated to bring buildings and parts of buildings to Dallas, such as the marble Indian pavilion in the Anatole hotel lobby. Still waiting to be placed is a pair of 10 foot high marble columns from the Yuan Ming Yuan summer palace in China. This love of strong shapes moulded in the round, "noble forms," runs throughout the collection. The jades, while small in scale, typify the "noble form," with qualities of structural elegance far beyond their size, even achieving a sort of grandeur. They are the core of the collection, the passion of passions.

The collection is unusual in that while every piece shows the influence of Trammell Crow, it does not all belong to him. Some pieces belong to him, others to his children, others to partnerships and companies. He has applied to oriental art the same philosophy with which he built his business: "I would rather own part of two, than all of just one."

This greatly complicated the preparation of this book, a gift to him and his wife Margaret from their six children.

"Salt and pepper" Siberian nephrite

months, or even years to complete. But the hardness of jade lends itself to fine sculptural effects. It can be cut paper thin, with soft curvings or sharp facets, and polished to a high luster—qualities shared by no other stone.

Jade in its pure form is not green, but white. "One should regard those white in color as the best," says the *Ge Gu Yao Lun*, the Ming collector's handbook. A flat white, called "mutton-fat" white, was highly valued, being used at court for pendants and imperial seals.

The colors of jade come from traces of other minerals in the stone. The most common colors are shades of green from pale celadon to almost black, yellow, brown, blue, gray, and lavender. "Red as a cock's comb, yellow as steamed millet,

"Spinach green" nephrite

Lavender jadeite

Sea green jadeite

"Moss entangled in snow" jadeite

Iridescent white jadeite

white as sliced lard, black as unmixed lacquer," was an old saying. Actually, there is no true red jade, red pieces usually turning out to be agate. But the reddish-brown crust of the jade boulder may feature in a sculpture, the russet skin accenting the green or white interior.

"The Chinese eye, and Chinese hands, seem in the past to have been capable of drawing from matter, any matter, charmed beauty that is unrivaled," wrote George Kates. The Chinese were fascinated with natural materials, with grain, texture, and the flow from one color to another. In jade, this resulted in carvings which made skillful use of color contrasts within the stone: emerald insects crawl on a brown leaf, green gourds hang from a white trellis on which alights a gray butterfly.

To some degree this play of colors was born of necessity. The jade boulder arrives at market with only a few square inches of surface removed. Even the most experienced carver can merely guess at the treasures within. Only as he begins to carve will the colors of the stone manifest themselves.

The Three Golden Ages

Jade carving had three golden ages. The first was characterized by the ritual jades of the late Shang dynasty (1766 BC-1122 BC) and Zhou dynasty (1122 BC-255 BC), the so-called "archaic" jades. These carvings, related to early bronzes, are magic talismans linking man to the gods. The ancients used them in court ceremonies and buried them with the dead. Their stark geometric shapes inscribed with animal patterns conjure up the high classic culture which produced the rites of kingship and the philosophies of Daoism and Confucianism.

The second great age was the Ming dynasty (1368 AD-1644 AD), when carvers achieved a new level of mastery over the material. From this era date refined vessels in scholarly taste, and the famous animals, full and rounded like jade boulders, but at the same time alert with the spark of life.

The greatest age was the reign of the Qianlong Emperor (1736 AD-1796 AD) of the Qing dynasty. Qianlong's reign was a prosperous age, the last great flowering of traditional Chinese culture, when literature and the arts flourished under an enlightened ruler.

The Qianlong jades, while lighter and more decorative than the sober works of the Ming, reach a high point of elegance and creative invention. The eclectic Qianlong artists took motifs from all periods and combined them in graceful sculptures in archaistic style. This was also the period of paper-thin Moghul style carvings, and the arrival of the new material of jadeite.

Jade in Chinese Culture

The survival of neolithic jade artifacts from sites as early as 6500 BC show that jade was considered precious long before written history. This attitude never changed. Recently a Tang dynasty (618 AD-907 AD) tomb was excavated in which a man was buried with all his wordly wealth, including an uncarved block of jade in the place of gold and silver bars.

Jade was valued for its hardness, its translucence, its colors, and its soft tactile qualities. The word became a synonym for "precious" or "noble," being used in expressions of polite discourse such as "jade hall" for a friend's house, or "jade gold music" for his singing. In a letter you requested a "jade reply" and at a business discussion you ended hopefully by saying, "I hope that you will be able to make this rough stone into jade."

Jade made its way into literature, art, and philosophy, adapting to different casts of mind and different ages. For the Confucianists, so concerned about propriety and ancient ritual, jade was the link to the sage kings of old. Confucius, it is related, played on the jade chime with such intensity that a passer-by remarked, "His heart is full who beats the jade musical stone."

Confucianism was the moral and scholarly backbone of the state. Jade, in the form of seals and archaistic objects, symbolized the legitimacy of the empire and its unbroken link to ages past.

Daoism, on the other hand, was the world of freedom from rules and rituals. The Daoists believed in a mysterious force infusing the universe called the *Dao*. Life was a wandering through a world of free-flowing forms, what the philosopher Zhuang-zi used to call, "the wanderings of the truth-picker."

The movement of the *Dao* could be seen in the shapes of rocks, rising smoke, and mushrooms. From Daoism, jade carvers took the love of natural boulder and pebble shapes. Also from Daoism are sinuous dragons, spiraling vines, and fertile peaches, all growing and changing, alive with the breath of the *Dao*.

Thus jade in its various forms came to represent the highest ideals of Chinese culture. Jade meant all that was most noble and beautiful. This is why the *Shuo Wen* dictionary, in the famous first definition of jade, phrased it so simply:

"Jade: The fairest of stones."

Opposite page:
Gu vase, pale green-white nephrite, Qing, Qianlong period [1736-1795], H 9 L 9 W 3.9 in.

The vase derives from the archaic *Gu* beaker, a bronze shape flaring upwards and downwards from a central node. The body formed of elongated lotus petals is almost eggshell thin, undercut at the base. At the center, is a flying *Apsara* (heavenly musician) in light relief, while at the sides, loose rings hang from hibiscus leaves. The *Apsara*, the lotus, and the hibiscus are all Buddhist symbols.

Archaic

Cong, mottled gray and brown nephrite, late Zhou, 4th-3rd century BC, H 2.75 W 1.5 in.

Inside the tube, the boring from top and bottom does not quite meet, a common feature in archaic *cong*.

Opposite page:

Cong, brownish-green partly calcinated nephrite, Han, 2nd century BC-1st century AD, H 8.25 W 4.5 in.

"Straight, square, great. Without purpose. Yet nothing remains unperfected." (*I Ching*)

Human history typically progressed from the Stone Age, to the Bronze Age, to the Iron Age. But some scholars have postulated another stage: the Jade Age. In China, New Zealand, and Pre-Columbian America, neolithic man found jade, and with it came significant advances in culture.

Jade's strength and durability made it a cutting tool superior to all other stones. Thus, the earliest Chinese daggers, saws, and axes were made of jade. Even until modern times, the carving of jade involved extreme concentration of labor, hence it was natural for jade to become an object of wonder, even of religious reverence. "Heaven is jade," says the I Ching, China's oldest book.

In time, the cutting tools lost their function and took on a religious and sacrificial character. In the Shang dynasty (1766 BC-1122 BC), new, purely symbolic shapes developed, and with them the cult of the dead. It became the custom to place jade in the tombs of kings and nobles. Jade was precious, like gold, and thought to have magical properties to protect against decomposition.

By the late Neolithic period, the Chinese had already formulated the beginnings of Daoism and the belief in Yin-Yang. Yang, the male principle, stands for heaven, roundness, the creative. Yin, the female principle, stands for earth, squareness, the receptive.

The Daoist sage Zhuang-zi writes: "Perfect Yin is stern and frigid. Perfect Yang is bright and glittering. The two mingle, penetrate, come together, harmonize, and all things are born therefrom. Perhaps someone manipulates the cords that draw it all together, but no one has ever seen his form."

These principles took concrete shape in two jade artifacts: the *Bi* disk and the *Cong* tube. The *Bi* disk, a circle with a hole in the middle, stood for the sun, for heaven. The *Cong*, a squared tube, stood for earth.

8

Bi Disks and Hu Blades

Reverse

The decoration falls into two circuits: the outer with Han style volutes and hatchwork, the inner with archaic "rice pattern" studs, such as are found on the most ancient *Bi*.

The *Bi* disk is the premier ritual object. People of ancient times deposited it in graves and laid it at the cornerstones of palaces. It symbolized heaven, and was one of the insignia of royalty. In later times, the *Bi* became a favorite theme of court and scholars, recreated in countless versions, large and small.

The *Hu* blade likewise had a long history. It began as a neolithic cutting tool, but by Han times (200 BC) it had become a mark of rank. Courtiers wore *Hu* blades tied by cords around their waists. This form disappeared in time, but its echo remains in the *Gui* scepter of later periods.

Bi disk, mottled gray nephrite, Song, 11th-13th century, 8 in. diam.

The *Bi* disk is in Song archaistic style, with dragons plunging in and out of a sea of clouds. By the time this piece was fashioned, the Shang ritual culture was long dead. Courtiers and literati used elaborate *Bi* as reminders of the past.

Opposite page:
Hu blade, green nephrite, Shang-Zhou, 13th-10th century BC, L 16.25 W 4.5 in.

The *Hu* blade served originally as a slicing tool, this one with its blade still razor sharp after three millennia. The drilled holes are for attachment to a handle, and later, when this tool became court regalia, for cords to be tied to the waist.

Gui scepter, greenish-white and brown nephrite, late Ming, early 17th century, H 13.75 in.

Five dragons writhing amidst clouds envelope the pointed rectangle shape, within which are medallions with calligraphy in ancient seal script.

Archaism

"A wide knowledge of antiquities is the first requisite of the gentleman," begins the preface of the *Ge Gu Yao Lun*, the Ming essay on connoisseurship. One trait of Chinese culture is its strong archaistic tendency, artists and scholars in every age turning to the past for inspiration. As a result, there was a continuity of form and style unique in world history.

The archaic shapes above all conjure up ritual. For the Chinese, "The Rites" were the basis of civilization. When one of Confucius' disciples tried to do away with the offering of a sheep for the ritual, Confucius retorted, "You love the sheep, I love the ceremony!"

Artifacts in the shape of ritual objects reminded men of ancient greatness, and symbolized a bond with the gods. To this day an archaistic form affects the educated Chinese like a bell echoing back through the years.

The evolution of the *Gui* scepter illustrates the process of archaism. Ancient axes and *Hu* blades began as cutting tools. By the Zhou dynasty (1122 BC-221 BC), they had developed into the *Gui* scepter, a symbol of rank interred with the dead. The *Gui* is a pointed rectangle. In time it replaced the *Cong* as complement to the *Bi* disk, becoming a new yin-yang, male-female pair.

In the Han dynasty (206 BC-220 AD), the *Gui* shrank in size, becoming rounded and portable for use at court. Sixteen hundred years later, at the end of the Ming dynasty (1368 AD-1644 AD), the *Gui* had become purely decorative. It was no longer carried; it stood upright, elaborately carved with calligraphy and encircling dragons.

Gui scepter, brown nephrite, Former Han, 3rd-2nd century BC, H 8.75 W 1.75 in.

The two holes are for suspending at the waist. Officials carried *Gui* scepters at palace functions, raising them before their faces as they spoke. This shape, with tapered sides and rounded end, has survived intact in the Shinto rites of modern Japan.

The Tao-Tie Mask

One of the enigmatic features of Chinese bronzes is the monster mask found on so many ancient pieces. Song scholars dubbed these masks the *Tao-tie*, or "Glutton." Nobody knows for sure what animal the *Tao-tie* represents: tiger, or ox, or dragon. But the theme has persisted until modern times, especially in archaistic jades.

The *Tao-tie* mask is highly abstract, with a tendency towards "animal interlace": parts of the body flow into one another. An eye becomes a claw; an eyebrow becomes a tail; the whole mask may be reversible, reading upside-down as well as right-side up.

Green jadeite vase, Qing, early 19th century, H 18 in. (detail)

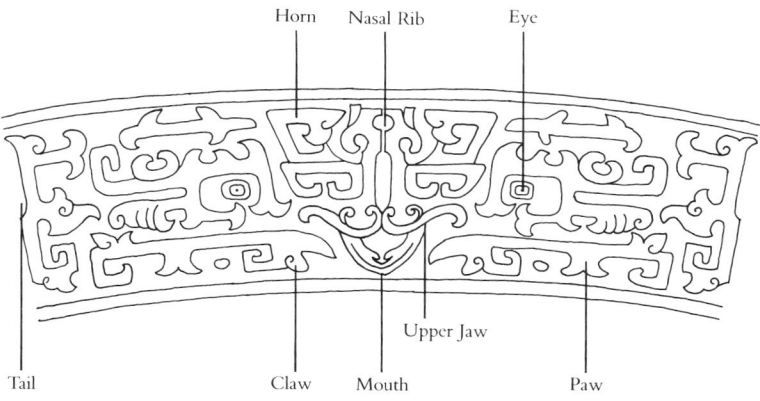

Simplification

"When the small man goes wrong, it is always on the side of over-elaboration," said Confucius. There has always been a stern side to Chinese aesthetics, rejecting ornament, and reducing objects to pure form.

Early bronzes represented the classic ideal, but they tended to be encrusted with complex patterns. Later collectors developed a taste for simplicity evident in the stark lines of Ming furniture, or Qing monochrome pottery. Here, the jade carver has used jade of purest white for a simplified version of the ancient bronze vessel *Dou*.

"Here at the highest stage of development," says the commentary to the I Ching, "all ornament is discarded. Perfect grace consists not in exterior ornamentation, but in the simple fitness of its form."

Dou vase, mutton-fat white nephrite, Qing, Qianlong period [1736-1795], H 6 W 6 in.

The ancient *Dou* would have had a lid and incised decoration. The jade carver has removed the lid and streamlined the form in order to show the high quality of white jade to best advantage.

Elaboration

"Ornament is great power indeed. It is born together with heaven and earth," says Liu Xie, the 6th century literary critic. For Liu Xie, the nature of human creativity lay in its ability to ornament, and he called this ability "the carving of dragons." One approach to art involved elaboration of antique form.

In the case of jade, this sometimes meant quite literally "the carving of dragons." In this piece, the carver has taken an old bronze libation vessel, the *Guang*, and added dragons climbing up the side.

The vase typifies one of the unique effects of jade carving: vessels entwined with life. Vessels come alive as dragons crawl over them, vines circle around them, or they sprout out of the backs of birds and animals. Just as a sunken pot becomes one with coral and sea life, jade vessels become one with plants and animals. "Is anyone responsible?" asks Liu Xie, "No. They are natural, organic expressions of the Divine."

Guang libation vessel, white nephrite with calcination, late Ming, 16th-17th century, H 9.5 W 6.5 in.

In this classic version of the archaistic taste, the carver has embellished the *Guang* shape with monster heads with loose rings in their mouths, and a *Chi* dragon climbing up the handle.

Natural Boulders

In opposition to the formal world of Confucian ritual, there always existed an alternative: Daoism, with its belief in nature and freedom. For the Daoists, the greatest beauty lay in leaving objects untouched. "If we must use compass and square to make something right, this means cutting away its inborn nature," said Zhuang-zi.

The shapes of stones contained the *Dao*, the "Way" of the universe. "The purest essence of the energy of the heaven-earth world coalesces into rock," begins a Song stone catalogue. This philosophy expressed itself in a fascination with jade in its natural state: boulders from the river bed.

A jade boulder consists of a core of jade covered by a brown oxidized "skin." Jade carvers would utilize the natural shape of the boulder to create small universes within. The interest in the skin of the boulder as well as the jade interior, led carvers to play with colors and textures. Later carvings show skillful use of the skin as a color accent.

Jade pebbles in the bed of the White Jade River near Khotan, Xinjiang Province in western China. (Photo: Fred Ward)

Opposite page:
Carved boulder, celadon nephrite with russet skin, Qing, Qianlong period [1736-1795], H 19 in.

The boulder is carved in deep relief with scholars gathered in a glade amid twisted pine trees and jagged rockwork, the skin carved in cloud patterns. With high quality celadon jade such as this, it is a great luxury to leave so much of the surface in the form of the brown "skin."

Carved boulder, celadon nephrite, Qing, Qianlong period [1736-1795], H 9.5 W 6 in.

The scene shows a *Lohan* (Buddhist adept) seated outside a grotto. Beside him a *ling-zhi* mushroom sprouts from a tripod cauldron; below him are his sandals. The poem on the rock reads:

"Wearing clothes with countless patches, holding a bamboo stick and the Buddha's scriptures, the *Acharya* (Perfected One) views his spirit within his breast. Suppose there is something written here: This writing is not the true void, for words are not necessary."

Reverse

Opposite page: *Carved boulder*, reverse. The free-hanging vines, steps, and rock plateau give an illusion of depth to the relief carving.

Carved boulder, light green nephrite, Qing, Qianlong period [1736-1795], H 7 W 15 in.

Massively carved with rocks overhanging figures descending into a cave, the boulder bears inscriptions commemorating two visits by the Qianlong emperor when he viewed this carving.

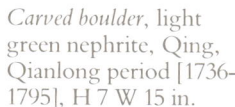

Pebbles

There is a story that the Emperor once ordered a jade artist to carve a dragon from a particularly fine pebble. But the artist returned the pebble saying he could find no dragon in it, only four carp swimming through a pool. The Emperor allowed the artist to sculpt the carp. But when he demanded the return of the excess jade cut away to make the carving, there was not enough dust to cover the palm of the Emperor's hand.

Jade boulders and pebbles intrigue because their brown skins give no clue to the treasures within. The *Shuo Wen* dictionary (ca. 100 AD) equates the ability to understand the interior of a jade pebble merely by looking at the outside with *Yi*, the virtue

Fu lion, calcined mottled nephrite, Ming, 16th-17th century, W 2.25 in.

The *Fu* lion rides on a cluster of swirling clouds, holding a branch of *Lingzhi* mushroom in its mouth.

Inscribed pebble, white nephrite, Qing, Qianlong period [1736-1795], H 4.25 W 6 in.

The pebble has lost its skin but is otherwise almost untouched, except for a lightly inscribed poem in seal script.

of understanding and right action in human affairs.

Pebbles are a delight because they can be felt as well as seen. Gentlemen of old China often carried carved jade pebbles worn and glossy from years of handling. "Warm and mellow," says a Ming collector, "one can feel when one fingers them, as if some unearthly stream is flowing into one's hand."

Pebble with carved landscape, gray-green nephrite with russet skin, Qing, ca. 1800, H 5.25 in.

An example of a microcosm in a small space: two figures stand in a rocky grotto above an acolyte in a smaller cave beside a pine tree. "Within the size of a fist can be assembled the beauty of a thousand cliffs." (*Song stone catalogue*)

Heavenly Twins, celadon nephrite, Qing, Qianlong period [1736-1795], H 3.5 W 4.5 in.

The box in one boy's hand, and the lotus at the shoulder of the other have several layers of meaning. The pronunciation of box (*He*) and lotus (*He*) both rhyme with *He*, meaning "Concord." At the same time they signify that these boys are the *Hehe*, the Heavenly Twins, gods guarding the door of the household.

21

Buddha's hand citron, celadon and russet nephrite, Qing, Qianlong period [1736-1795], H 8 in.

A deeply hollowed fruit with long curling fingers rises above a leafy twig spray coiling from the base. The Buddha's Hand, the peach, and the pomegranate, are the three auspicious fruit known as the "Three Abundances".

Plants

For the Chinese, all of nature is alive with a primal energy called *qi*. *Qi* flows through people and things, making them move, grow, and decay. For example, a mountain ridge twists like a dragon and breathes mists. The great artist is able to capture the *qi* as it flows; a great artwork must be infused with this breath of life.

Plants exemplify the flowing *qi*, especially spreading plum branches, climbing vines, and the budding fingers of the fruit known as the Buddha's hand citron. In jade carving all of nature partakes of this flow, one animal dissolving into another animal, and then branching like a plant. The tails of *Chi* dragons fork like vines; wings become mushrooms; mushrooms become bats.

In addition to the flow from form to form, the Chinese delighted in the flow of meanings: from object to symbol. Thus, objects came to stand for their rhymes. The Buddha's hand citron, for example, pronounced *Fu shou*, rhymes with *Fu* meaning happiness and *Shou* meaning long life.

The use of an object as a pun on meaning is called a rebus. The rebus had a profound impact on jade carving. Very often, a carving contains a "secret message" only to be unlocked by an understanding of its rebus.

Trellis, white, green, and gray-black jadeite, ca. 1920. H 5.75 W 5 in.

Vines and gourds hang from a trellis. The carving makes expert use of colors, bringing green into the gourds and gray-black into the butterfly. There is a rebus here: the word for melon is *Wan* while the word for vine is *Dai*. Together they signify *Wandai*; meaning "ten thousand generations," implying wishes for long life, many children, etc.

Brush rest, white mutton fat nephrite, Qing, Qianlong period [1736-1795], W 5.75 in.

An example of the flow of forms, the brush rest is in the form of a dragon, except that the head and limbs of the dragon are mushrooms, and the body is a stalk. "Plants produce leopards and leopards produce horses and horses produce men. Men in time return again to the mysterious workings. So all creatures come out of the mysterious workings and go back into them again." says Zhuang-zi.

Imperial seal, dark green nephrite, Qing, Yongzheng period [1723-1736], H 3.75 W 5.06 in.

The seal, a gift to Emperor Yongzheng from his subjects, bears an inscription in Chinese and Manchu praising the Emperor.

Imperial seal, green nephrite, Qing, Qianlong, dated 1793, H 5.5 W 3.75 in.

The six-character seal reads: "Treasure of the Old Man of Absolute Fulfillments." The inscription, dated 1793, is from a composition by Emperor Qianlong, later published in 1810. Qianlong writes:

"On reaching the age of eighty I adopted the motto: 'Unceasingly he seeks to improve himself' for my self-encouragement Whether I can live up to this motto, I cannot tell . . . but thus I shall faithfully await Heaven's permission to approach the realm of absolute fulfillments by doing, during the next three years, as much as can be done during thirty years. How fortunate that would be!"

Government and Ritual

With a history reaching back into the Stone Age, jade became the patent of authority. Ministers wore jade pendants signifying rank, and carried jade scepters. Jade plaques commemorated laws and ceremonies; jade seals stamped state documents.

The mantic power of the seal in China and Japan is as strong, or maybe stronger, than the signature in the West. Scholars possessed many seals carved with their names, artist's sobriquets, and literary mottos. Collectors added their seals to paintings and calligraphy. Under the Qing dynasty, the punishment for forging an imperial seal was death. In the Imperial Palace, the seals stood in rows on raised pedestals in a special throne room of their own.

Premier amongst the Imperial Seals was the legendary "Seal Transmitting the State," handed down through the dynasties since the Zhou period. Many times lost, it was recovered by successive emperors and symbolized the "Mandate of Heaven." At the end of the Qing Dynasty in 1912, this mythical seal was again lost, its whereabouts today unknown.

Book plate, green nephrite, Qing, 18th century, H 11.1 W 4 in.

The inscription, in blue and gilt, is in Manchu, a Mongolian-type script used by the Qing imperial house. By the late 18th century, Manchu was no longer a living script, but was kept alive for ritual purposes by the Qing government. On the underside of this plaque are slits for thongs to bind to a book, probably a book of Buddhist sutras.

Imperial seal, pale celadon nephrite, Qing, Yongzheng period [1736–1795], H 6.7 W 6 in.

The seal, carved from the highest quality pale celadon nephrite, reads: *Yang Xin Shi Bao*, "Treasure of the Chamber of Cultivating Mind." The name is inspired by the Yang Xin Dian, "Hall of Cultivating Mind," the residence of the Qing emperors inside the Forbidden City.

According to former owners, this seal was taken from the Yuan Ming Yuan Summer Palace during the sack by Western powers in the 19th century.

God of the Southern Pole Star, painting on silk, Qing, early 18th century, H 84.5 W 47 in.

The God of the Southern Pole Star (god of immortality) stands with the immortal Zhong-li Quan, and attendants. The red ball on his headpiece signifies a star deity. The boy is holding a sprig of *Ling-zhi* mushroom, while the immortal grasps a crooked wooden staff. The combination of the spirit mushroom and the magic staff became the *Ruyi* scepter.

Opposite page:

Ruyi scepter, green-black nephrite, Qing, Qianlong period [1736-1795], H 1.25 W 3 L 13 in.

This *Ruyi* takes the shape of a gnarled branch, with mushrooms, peaches, and a pair of bats in low relief.

Ruyi scepter, green nephrite, Qing, early 19th century, L 15.5 in.

Three bats on the body, and a stylized *Shou* (Immortality) character on each of the three medallions indicate wishes for good fortune and long life.

Ruyi scepter, pale celadon nephrite, Qing, mid-19th century, L 18 in.

This *Ruyi* was a gift to celebrate a birthday. The three panels portray immortals carrying fans, peaches, and mushrooms, all symbolizing long life.

Ruyi Scepters

The word *Ruyi* means literally "As you like." In contrast to the sharp lines of the *Gui* scepter, the Daoists created their own scepter, in the freeform shape of a *Ling-zhi* mushroom. The *Ruyi* scepter is formed by two arcs meeting at a raised central point, topped with a turned-back head.

The *Ruyi* became the mark of Daoist and Buddhist sages. Eventually it entered the court where it served many functions: symbol of rank, auspicious gift, decoration. *Ruyi* exist in an infinity of styles and materials. The more formal pieces clearly show the two arcs and three medallions (the head, the raised center, and the foot), while others are contorted branches sprouting mushrooms and peaches.

The *Ling-zhi*, meaning "spirit mushroom" is a favorite Chinese theme because of its medicinal qualities, thought to ensure immortality. The outspreading mushroom heads symbolize the flow of the *Dao*, like rising smoke and waves. Scholars would decorate their studios with pots of *Ling-zhi* mushrooms. As a design motif, the convolutions of its shape appealed to the age-old fascination with spirals, such as are found on archaic bronzes.

After the development of *Ruyi* scepters, the mushroom shape itself came to be called *Ruyi*, often used as a rebus meaning "As you like." Another popular rebus found on *Ruyi* scepters is the bat. The word for bat, *Fu*, rhymes with *Fu* meaning "good fortune." Thus a bat on a *Ruyi* signifies: "Good fortune as much as you like."

Musical Stones

Zhong Bell, white nephrite with brown and black inclusions, Qing, early 19th century, H 7 W 5.62 in.

Court music also made use of a set of *Zhong* bronze bells, graduated in size like the jade chimes. This version in jade is decorative, not functional. But the *Tao-tie* mask and classic bronze shape, combined with brown and black mottlings in the stone, create an archaistic flavor.

"When the early rulers formed Music, their purpose was not to satisfy the senses, but rather to bring the people back to the correct direction in life," says the ancient Book of Music. The Chinese saw music not as beautiful or ugly, but as moral or immoral. It was vital for the health of the state that the proper music be played.

For this purpose the court maintained sets of jade chimes, called *Qing*. The *Qing*, shaped like a carpenter's square, came in two types: the *Bien Qing*, sets of 16 or 24, depending on the dynasty, and the *Te Qing*, one large stone struck at the end of a chant or hymn.

The sound of the *Qing* had the magical power to transform men's hearts for the good. "He who could fully comprehend this ceremony," says Confucius, "could rule the world as though it were spinning on his hand."

Because the *Qing* was so powerful and auspicious, and because it rhymes with *Qing* meaning "Congratulations," it became a popular rebus used as a decorative motif.

28

Te Qing Chime, green nephrite with calcination at one end, Qing, 17th century, L 21.75

This chime is the solitary *Te Qing* which played one note at the end of the verse to "receive the sound." Larger than most *Qing* existing today, it dates from before the Qianlong period, when *Qing* were standardized in a smaller size.

Single *Te Qing* jade chime

Set of 16 *Bien Qing* jade chimes

Decorative Qing Chime, pale-green jadeite, late Qing, ca. 1880, L 12 in.

Purely auspicious and decorative, the chime is carved with archaistic dragons on the top, clouds on the bottom, and three medallions with the character *Shou* (long life).

Incense

Ding censer, celadon and brown nephrite, Qing, Qianlong period [1736-1795], H 7.25 W 9.5 in.

The carver has modified the basic *Ding* shape by adding a reticulated dome cover and a *Tao-tie* mask on the body, and by changing the handles, originally upturned, into monster heads with rings hanging from their mouths.

Incense for the Chinese appeals to all the senses, not just one.

Fragrance has mystery because it affects the sense of smell, the deepest layer of the brain. Incense reaches to a level below conscious thought, and is therefore used in religious rituals all over the world.

The clouds of rising smoke fascinate the eye because the swirling wisps reveal the patterns of the *Dao*, like waves or mountain peaks. The earliest censers actually took the shape of rising mountains.

Even the ears become involved, for the act of concentrating on a smell is like listening. A whiff of incense is as powerful as a sound. "In a jade brazier charcoal burns: perfumed drum-beats," writes the Tang poet Li He.

Incense being central to ritual, incense burners are the most archaistic of all vessels. The favorite shape is the *Ding*, the divine tripod. The *Ding*, originally a food container, is the oldest of all the bronze shapes. Shang emperors used it in the sacrifices to the supreme deity as early as the 15th century BC. The very word is auspicious, the symbol of all that is highest in civilization. "The *Ding* has rings of jade. Great good fortune," proclaims the *I Ching*.

Three Piece Sets

The full incense ceremony required a set of three vessels, the *San-shi*. These are:

(1) *A container for incense.* Traditional incense was not in the form of tall sticks as are commonly used today. The low, lidded box would contain slivers of sandalwood, chips of rare Burmese aloes, or perhaps small buttons of incense made from aromatic powders. To this day the custom of displaying the incense container survives in the Japanese tea ceremony.

(2) *A vase for tongs and spatula.* Before burning incense, the owner used the spatula to flatten and mold the ash. He would then take the tongs, deposit charcoal in the ash and place a sliver of incense on the charcoal.

(3) *The censer.* Usually in the shape of an archaic bronze vessel, the incense burner had a lid to protect the ash. A reticulated lid allowed the incense to burn without having to remove the lid.

Incense Set, mutton fat white nephrite on carved wooden base, Qing, Qianlong period [1736-1795], Overall H 14 in.

The set is in archaic taste, the vessels carved with flanges at the edges like ancient bronzes. The incense burner is a *Fang Ding*, a square *Ding*, with four legs and the characteristic high-rising handles. The vase is a *Fang Gu*, a square *Gu* flaring upwards and downwards from a central node. The box is also squared off in matching style.

Incense Set, spinach-green nephrite, Qing, Qianlong period [1736-1795], Tallest H 9.5 in.

Five-clawed imperial dragons writhe amidst stylized cloud scrolls completely covering all three pieces, of unusually large size. The clouds on the spatula create cloud patterns on the surface of the ash inside the censer.

Censer, rare blue jadeite with pale and russet inclusions, Qing, 19th century, W 7.5 in.

The censer is a highly modified *Ding* tripod, with lion-mask handles suspending loose rings, a high domed cover with four small loose ring handles, and a coiled dragon finial.

Opposite page:

Pair of incense containers, white nephrite with green bases, Qing, 18th century, H 12.5 in.

Tubes like these housed perfume incense sticks. The perforations allow perfume to escape and scent the surroundings.

Pair of incense containers, green nephrite with white bases, Qing, 19th century, H 8.75 in.

Three Rams, russet and grayish green nephrite, Ming, 16th-17th century, H 3 W 5 in.

The parent sits with two lambs, each with its head turned over its shoulder. The ram, pronounced *Yang*, is a rebus for *Yang*, the male principle.

Dog, white nephrite with russet inclusions, Song, 11th-13th century, H 1.35 W 2.35 in.

This early carving captures a dog's plaintive loyalty, in an atmosphere of quiet.

Animals and Birds

From the first, jade animals showed the influence of pebbles. They hold their limbs close to their bodies, their heads turn back over their shoulders, and they tend to remain seated. Animals only got up off their feet in the Ming dynasty.

The early Han animals open their mouths wide, their bodies tensed as though responding to other animals. But by Tang and Song times the animals have relaxed. They sit, like the Song dog with crossed paws illustrated here, infused with that special quality of Chinese animals: alive, alert, yet utterly calm.

Birds came even later than animals. They reached their heyday in the 19th century when the carvers discovered jadeite. The bright hues of jadeite lent themselves to brilliant plumage, and the technical mastery of the period allowed carvers to explore new effects.

Animals are nature in a mischievous mood. When animals take over, the world goes topsy-turvy, as in the Ming novel *Journey to the West*:

"Tigers will sit in the music rooms,
Wolves will be in charge of the accounts.
Lions and elephants will be kings,
With tigers and leopards for ministers.
A wild boar will carry your luggage,
And a water monster will lead the way."

Camel, green-gray nephrite, early Qing, 17th century, W 12.5 in.

The camel is the fabled beast of Central Asia, source of most Chinese jade until modern times. Although the head stands free, the sculpture is very simple, virtually a polished pebble.

Horse, celadon nephrite, Ming, 16th century, H 8 W 5.5 in.

Animal carving reached a high point in the Ming Dynasty with large reclining sculptures of horses and water buffalo. This horse is thought to come from the Yuan Ming Yuan summer palace near Beijing. The piece integrates massive volume with delicately carved mane, tail, and outlined lips.

Elephant, white nephrite with dark green jadeite caparison and tusks, late Qing, ca. 1910, H 10.75 W 13 in.

The elephant, coming from India, is associated with Buddhism. This elephant originally supported a statue of a Buddhist deity. The caparison is decorated with a *Shou* character (meaning "long life"), bats (*Fu*, rhyming with "good fortune"), and ocean waves. The rebus means: "May you have life as long lasting as the southern mountains; may your good fortune be broad as the sea."

The two-tier stand, made of gilt bronze and enamel, with carved jade balustrades and white jade plaques, is the hallmark of a noted jade carver of the late Qing.

Elephant, gray and brown nephrite, Ming – Qing, 17th century, W 8.25 in.

The downcast head rests upon the curled trunk, and the tusks are short. In contrast to the sharp lines of the standing green elephant, this elephant is only a few incisions away from rounded pebble.

Elephant, laurel green nephrite, Qing, Yongzheng period [1723-1736], H 10.5 in.

This elephant, cut from stone similar to the Yongzheng imperial seal; (p. 24), is from a famous and controversial group of animals. It was illustrated in the Qianlong jade catalogue *Gu Yu Tu Lu* as a Han work.

Today scholars believe this and the other animals in the group (a horse, a tiger, a monkey, and a water buffalo) to be early 18th century. All share the sculptural strength which gives this elephant a unique "modern" flavor.

Pair of phoenix vases, light lavender with apple green inclusions jadeite, Qing, late 19th century, H 12.25 in.

Gu vases rise from the backs of two phoenixes. The phoenix is magical and symbolizes the Empress, as the dragon symbolizes the Emperor. Its appearance was a good omen. Confucius complains about the decline of the times by commenting that the "phoenix is seen no more."

Two quail, white and brown nephrite, Qing, 18th-19th century, H 2.5 W 3 in.

Two quail bearing a sprig of millet play on a lotus leaf. "The quail go in pairs, the magpies fly two by two," a line from the *Shi Jing* anthology (1,000-600 BC), was much quoted as a political allegory.

Duck, white nephrite with brown spots, late Ming, 16th–17th century, W 8 in.

This duck resembles Ming animals: head turned back and wings held close to the body, thus preserving the shape of the original pebble.

The duck, usually shown with a spray of lotus in its beak symbolizes marital bliss, as the male and female always swim in pairs.

Rooster-form box, pale apple-green jadeite, Qing, mid-19th century, H 5 W 7 in.

A rooster holding a sprig of millet in its mouth watches over five chicks. The upper part of the carving is a lid, attached to the lower part by a loose chain. The theme of a rooster with five chicks is a reminder of the importance of a father educating his children.

Mythical Animals

Confucius stopped recording history at the point when the unicorn was captured in 481 BC. After that, say the commentators, there was nothing worth writing about.

Capturing the unicorn was sacrilege because the unicorn, the chimera, and other mythical animals are messengers of the gods and immortals.

Deer of the immortals, white nephrite with dark brown rivering, late Ming, 16th-17th century, H 3.25 in.

The deer of the immortals, with flames rising from his forelegs, carries in his mouth a sprig of the *Ling-zhi* mushroom, which, it is said, only he can find.

Fu lion, celadon nephrite, Qing, early 19th century, H 3.75 W 4 in.

Fu lions, a cross between lions and dogs, with squared-off muzzles and bulging eyes, often appear in pairs at the entrances to temples and palaces. The butterfly on his tail irritates the lion and causes him to dance and chase after it.

Chimera, gray-blue jadeite, Qing, 19th century, H 2.25 W 5.75 in.

The *Chimera* is a cross between a lion and a unicorn, with wings (symbolized by the flame scroll under the forelegs).

The mythical animals are composites born of the Chinese love of forms flowing into one another. The world of these beasts could be decidedly weird. As the Tang poet Li He describes them in a mediumistic poem:

"Blue raccoons are weeping blood,
As shivering foxes die.
Painted dragons on the wall with gold tails,
Rain-elves ride them away to autumn lakes.
A hundred year old owl becomes a tree-sprite
And the voice of laughter, jade-green fire, leaps from his nest."

Chimera vase, green nephrite, Qing, 19th century, H 9 W 6 in.

A square *Gu* vase rises from the back of a chimera. On his forelegs are tongues of flame, and behind them rise clouds, becoming wings, which open and turn into mushrooms.

The Dragon

"Flying transformations,
Coiling through the clouds.
These are the holy and
magical dragons,
Surrounding the palace with
numinous radiance"
(*Journey to the West*)

Dragon plaque, calcinated white nephrite, Ming-Ching, 16th-17th century, H 2.25 W 2.5 in.

This archaistic piece is modelled after the flat pendants of the Zhou period.

Pendant, white and russet nephrite, Qing. 17th century, H 2.12 W 2.9

The *Chi* dragon, a child dragon, has a feline head, a sinuous body without scales, rounded paws, and a tail which splits into two or three curling projections. It is popular as an archaistic design.

Censer lid, green nephrite, Qing, Qianlong period [1736-1795], H 8 W 9.5 in.

Two writhing dragons and phoenixes chase flaming pearls amongst clouds.

The dragon causes storms and rain, is king of the four seas, and possesses the wish-fulfilling gem. The dragon is the Emperor.

Dragons exist in many varieties: the *Kui* dragon, an abstract form found in animal interlace designs; the *Chi* dragon, a child dragon; the *Lung* dragon and *Mang* dragon, full-fledged Imperial dragons with scales, manes, whiskers, and talons; and other forms, with or without horns, wings, tiger's feet, or fins.

The dragon being an imperial symbol, sumptuary laws regulated its use. Only certain ranks of officials could display certain types of dragons, the 5-clawed and 3-clawed dragons being reserved for the Court. In 1537, an official enraged the Emperor by wearing a flying fish which resembled the Imperial dragon too closely.

The dragon is the symbol of the raw energy of nature. As a design motif, it affords the chance to explore the twisting, flowing forms so dear to the Chinese craftsman.

Dragonized carp, dark green nephrite, Qing, Qianlong period [1736-1795], H 8 in.

According to legend, the carps of the Yellow River which succeed in reaching the rapids of the Dragon Gate, are transformed into dragons. Carps rising out of the water became an analogy for literary success, promising honor and rewards for those who passed their examinations. This carving shows the carp at the moment of transformation.

Imperial seal, green nephrite, Qing, Qianlong period, 1796-1799, H 6.7 W 6 in.

The dragon on the top is the double-dragon of Imperial seals, seated and formal. The seal bears the Emperor Qianlong's title after retirement in 1796.

The Human Figure

The human figure came last in what has been called the "Chinese artist's gradual conquest of the universe."

First came geometry: the circles and trapezoids of *Bi* disks and *Hu* blades. Then came "animal interlace": abstract animal forms flowing into one another like the ancient *Tao-tie* masks. Following this came realistic animals and plants. And finally, as if jade carving had traced in miniature the course of earth's evolution, the artists reached man.

The human body per se plays only a small part in Chinese and Japanese art. Much of the interest in the human figure lies in the flowing patterns of draperies. *Apsaras*; the heavenly musicians of the Tang, waft long curling ribbons of gauze behind them as they fly through the sky. Emperors and immortals sit sternly with robes falling in stylized folds.

Faces are idealized, but highly expressive, especially the characterful faces of Daoist and Buddhist sages.

Brush washer, yellow nephrite, Ming, 16th century, H 3 W 3.25 in.

"Childlike folly brings good fortune," says the I Ching. Playing children is an auspicious theme in Chinese art. Two children face each other across a large jar, used as a scholar's brush washer, carved of rare yellow jade.

Opposite page: *Bodhidharma Crossing the Yangtse River on a Reed*, celadon nephrite blending into cream and sepia, Qing, late 18th-early 19th century, W 8.5 in.

Bodhidharma is the founder of Zen Buddhism. When he arrived at the court of southern China in the 6th century, the Emperor asked him, "I have built many temples and support many priests. According to Zen, what merit have I gained?" Bodhidharma replied, "No merit."

The Emperor was displeased, and Bodhidharma had to flee to the north, crossing the Yangtse river on a reed. This dialogue became a famous Zen *koan*, a thought on which to meditate. The title for the *koan* is "Bodhidharma on a reed."

Koans, like "What is the sound of one hand clapping?" are generally impossible to answer. The impossible question asked by this sculpture is: Why is doing good works without merit? And what is merit?

The Gods and Immortals China had two divine pantheons: Daoist and Buddhist. Buddhism, coming from India, emphasized renunciation of the world. There is the cosmic Buddha behind all appearance, the historical Buddha, and Buddhas of the past and future. Below these are *bodhisattvas*, divine beings who vow to work for the salvation of all sentient beings. On earth are hermits, such as the *Lohans* frequently pictured in Chinese art with their gnarled and wizened figures.

Pair of Guanyin, celadon nephrite, Qing, Qianlong period [1736–1795], H 6.25 W 4.25 in.

The Goddess Guanyin, "She Who Hears the Cries of the World" is the *bodhisattva* of compassion. Greatly beloved by the Chinese, images of Guanyin exist in every medium. Guanyin's hair is piled high and covered by the cowl which is her mark. She carries a scroll of Buddhist sutras in her hand.

"A jade face full of heavenly happiness,
She delivers from the eight disasters
And saves all living beings.
Great is her compassion
She rescues the suffering when she hears their cries
Never failing to answer every call,
Infinitely divine and miraculous"
 (*Journey to the West*)

It is said that each culture's heaven mirrors its political system. Daoism, native to China, took the form of a huge bureaucracy. Over all ruled the Jade Emperor, and under him were various boards, managed by civil and military ministers. These wrote memorials to the throne and maintained voluminous files, just like officials on earth.

Just as on earth there were men who opted out of the system and became sages, so there were immortals who stood outside the heavenly bureaucracy. These lived carefree lives in the Isles of Immortality and the Kun Lun mountains. They are depicted with thoughtful and whimsical expressions.

Immortal, pale green nephrite, Qing, Qianlong period [1736-1795], H 11 W 2.9 in.

An immortal with flowing beard stands calmly with hands clasped behind him.

"His hair was bound with a pair of silken bands
His flowing gown had two capacious sleeves
An eternal child amid the mountains,
Untouched by any speck of dust,
He let the years go tumbling by."
(*Journey to the West*)

Reverse

Courtly Life

The few objects illustrated here give a hint of the life in the Forbidden City in Beijing, splendor on a scale to defy the imagination. In the 1930's George Kates saw one of the palaces, locked up for decades, with its original objects intact. It was only a few chambers out of over 4,000 rooms. He communicates the sense of awe:

"There must have been vaster amounts here than I believe one could find in any similar Western palace... The Emperor, then, how had the Emperor felt? The Emperor of China in that time of prosperity had owned so many examples of every known object under heaven that paradoxically he became an almost propertyless man, moving everywhere and forever through an endless maze of almost impersonal possession... A nation of five hundred million, aesthetically talented, had for centuries been heaping up quantities of treasure, for every use and of every variety; all the best flowed regularly to the court, much of it even to the palace, for the use of this One Man... Perspectives of almost terrifying abnormality kept opening before me that afternoon."

Marriage bowl, dark green nephrite, Qing, early 19th century, H 3 W 13 in.

Alms bowl, yellow-white nephrite, Qing, Qianlong period [1736-1795], H 3.25 W 9 in.

In the palace, even the begging bowls of the Buddhist monks were exquisitely carved jade. "Thus," says the I Ching, "the superior man dispenses riches downward, and refrains from resting on his virtue."

Alms bowl, base

Dragon bowl, green and brown nephrite, late Ming, 17th century, W 11.25 D 9.5 in.

Four scaly five-clawed dragons fly amidst clouds.

The most famous vessel in the palace was a huge jade basin carved with dragons, dating back to Yuan times. Marco Polo noted it in his travels. The bowl was prince of the "dragon-bowl" type of which these are two examples.

From the inscription composed by Emperor Qianlong in honor of the great dragon bowl:

"The measureless spirit of creation drives through infinite chaos. Terrifying waves seethe and surge through a waste of loud contorted waters . . . Every monster of fable is among the creatures thronging the thunderous upsurging waters. The king of the *Chi* dragons looms purple . . . while scaly dragons abound, and scarlet dragons breathe fire . . . From all eternity nature manifests spirit wonders, sprouting up like clouds, and pressing down like vast oceans."

Dragon bowl, green and brown nephrite, Ming, 16th-17th century, H 2.5 W 10 in.

Five *Chi* dragons fly amidst clouds.

Shown here are humble objects of daily life, rendered in jade: an iron, a mirror, a pipe, a backscratcher, and a hat stand. Life in the palace was truly a life of jade:

"After the emperors had slept in their jade bed, held court from their jade thrones, delighted in their jade mountains and bowls, or admired their large jade animals, they turned to other objects in the precious stone . . . For out of doors, the emperor had his leather riding crop with white jade top, and his wooden one with both head and tip in that stone . . . If he wished to go for a stroll in the gardens, there were his five walking sticks with white jade handles and ferrules . . . Because the imperial tutor could not indicate the characters with his finger, he was equipped with a finely wrought, flawless white jade pointer one foot long . . . Jade chopsticks car-

ried the food from jade serving dishes to individual jade rice bowls. Jade spoons were used for soup, and jade handled knives cut the fruit."

Iron, bronze with white jadeite handle, late Qing, ca. 1900, H 4.5 L 13.5 in.

Mirror, repoussé silver inlaid with green jadeite, late Qing, ca. 1900, L 20 W 6.5 in.

Pipe, green nephrite body with white tips, gray flecked bowl, and enamelled metal, Qing, late 19th century, L 19 in.

Hat Stand, pale celadon nephrite embossed with rubies, Qing, Qianlong period [1736–1795], L 16 in.

This is one of a pair of stands for mandarin court hats.

Back Scratcher, green and white nephrite with inlaid hardstones, Qing, Qianlong period [1736–1795], L 10 in.

Carnelian and other precious stones accent the spiral handle, in Moghul Indian style.

Translucent Surface

The hardness of jade allows it to be cut to a glossy smoothness and transparency. The effect is like fine porcelain. Connoisseurs collected pairs of thinly carved bowls for their textures and radiant colors.

The desire to copy the luster of jade led Chinese potters to invent their most famous glaze: celadon, a pale green verging on blue. Celadon was the poor man's jade. But with the passage of centuries, the celadon porcelain of the Song dynasty came to be valued in its own right.

Pair of bowls, pale blue-green jadeite on wood stands, Qing, 19th century, H 2.25 W 5.5 in.

Pair of bowls, green jadeite, Qing, late 19th century, W 8 in.

So jade now copied celadon and other glazes. A fine piece of pale-green jade would be carved into a dish or cup to look like porcelain. China's long continuity of culture led to such enfoldings of life and art back upon themselves: Art copied life, which copied art, and back again.

Pair of bowls, mutton fat white nephrite, Qing, 18th–19th century, H 3.25 W 8.5 in.

Lightly incised gilded branches of plum blossoms disguise flaws in the stone.

Pair of bowls, green and white jadeite on ivory stands, Qing, 19th century, H 1.75 W 5 in.

These palace bowls are carved with Buddhist images in the Tibetan style patronized by the Manchu court. Inscribed in Tibetan is the Invocation to the Buddha, the Buddhist Law, and the Priesthood, followed by the title of the Sutra of the Previous Lives of the Buddha.

Following page:

Plate, pale celadon nephrite, Qing, Qianlong period [1736-1795], H 2 W 10.5 in.

Vessels

Jade was used for every conceivable container: boxes, tea cups, jars, flower vases, etc. The vessels fall into two main categories: variations on archaic bronze shapes, and imitations of flowers and fruit.

Qing archaism did not slavishly imitate the antique. Artisans ransacked the past for unusual shapes, out of which they created new shapes. An example of this is the color mixer of late Zhou. This form had disappeared for almost two thousand years until the Qing carvers rediscovered it.

Of fruit, the peach is the favorite form, and of flowers, it is the lotus. The peach, a symbol of longevity, is Daoist in inspiration. The lotus is sacred to Buddhism.

Box, dark green nephrite, Qing, 19th century, W 9 in.

Boxes like this, sometimes used as incense burners, are derived from late Zhou color mixers. The central band imitates bamboo lattice.

Lotus-form bowl, salt-and-pepper Siberian nephrite, Qing, Qianlong period [1736-1795], H 3.5 W 6.5 in.

This piece in the Moghul style consists of a bowl and lid in the form of lotus petals. Inside are three layers of petals where the lid and body meet. The lid handle is a half-tied knot with a loose ring.

Lotus-form vessel, celadon nephrite, late Qing, ca. 1900, H 7 W 7.5 in.

In the Moghul style, a stand of lotus and hibiscus petals supports a lotus-form bowl rising to a hollowed-out lotus bud.

Vases

Hu Vase, dark green nephrite, Qing, 19th century, H 14 W 8 in.

A *Fu* lion sits on the lid, and a loose rendering of a *Tao-tie* monster mask covers the central band.

Opposite page:

Bian Hu Vase, dark green nephrite inlaid with coral cabochons, Qing, Qianlong period [1736-1795], H 13.5 in.

The body is finely engraved with a lattice pattern outlined in gilding, the interstices set with small coral beads. On the shoulders are monster mask handles with rock crystal for eyes, and loose rings.

Of all archaic forms, the *Hu* vase had overwhelming popularity in porcelain and other media as well as jade.

The *Hu* vase, dating back to the 12th century BC, is the familiar Chinese vase shape, with low belly and elongated neck. The *Hu* came in variations such as the *Bian Hu* (flattened body), *Fang Hu* (squared body), and the *Ping* (with a flat base).

Reverse

Hu Vase, pale lavender jadeite, Qing, mid-late 19th century, H 7.5 W 4 in.

The vases are titled "The Three Friends of Winter" and decorated with the "three friends": bamboo, pine, and plum. Bamboo and pine keep their greenery throughout the winter. The plum tree blossoms in late winter, heralding the spring while snow is still on the ground.

Hanging Vases

Loose rings are a favorite jade technique. Artisans showed off their skills by cutting very delicate rings as on the *Gu* beaker (p. 7) and unusual loops as on the lid of the lotus-form bowl (p. 62).

The next step from rings was chains. Here jade carvers delighted in technical tours-de-force. They linked lids to containers, as in the rooster-form box (p. 43), and they suspended vases, musical stones, and bird sculptures from ingeniously carved chains, giving the solid material of jade a sense of airy lightness.

Hanging Hu Vase, moss green nephrite, late Qing, ca. 1900, H 14 W 4.75 in.

Unusual figure-eights link to form two chains hanging from a clappet of two dragon heads.

The Scholar

The famous first lines of the Confucian Analects begin: "Is it not pleasant to learn and study? Is it not delightful to have friends come from afar?"

No nation has ever valued scholarship as the Chinese did. As early as the first century AD they had established the examination system, the world's first civil service examinations. Until 1906, when the system was finally abolished, the only road to official position in China was through the examinations.

Candidates displayed their knowledge of history, philosophy, and literature, by writing the infamous "Eight-Legged Essays": essays in eight sections all in rhymed couplets, which at the same time must be masterworks of fine calligraphy.

Over the centuries, a scholarly culture grew up, with emphasis on literature and art.

The Song calligrapher Huang Tingjian used to say that "a scholar would wither away if for more than three days he was not 'watered' by ancient writings." So strong was this tradition, that sometimes it was more important that an official have good taste in paintings and good handwriting than that he govern properly.

Above all, the scholars loved their studios, centered around the "Four Treasures": ink stick, ink stone, brush, and paper. In addition, there were numerous other utensils of the scholar's desk, all of which became works of art in their own right: brush pots, paperweights and scroll weights, water drippers, seals, brush washers, etc. These were fashioned of every material; porcelain, wood, bamboo, lacquer, stone, bronze, and frequently, jade.

Brush pot, celadon nephrite with brown inclusions, Qing, 18th century, H 7.06 W 7.12 in.

Six brushes, green and white nephrite, and green jadeite, 18th - 20th century, L in. (14" largest), L in. (6.5" smallest)

"The brush's value is certainly not less, and may be more, than that of a fishing net, a plough, a bow or arrow, a pestle or mortar, a boat or raft, a palace." (*Ming collector*)

Scholar's rock, volcanic stone, Qing, 19th century, H 4.75 in.

Although not jade, such rocks, valued for their strange shapes, appealed to the same taste which appreciated jade pebbles. Scholars kept rocks or "spirit stones" on their tables to remind them of the workings of the Dao.

Circular box, white nephrite, Qing, 17th-19th century, H 1 D 2 in.

The Ming scholars believed in simplicity. The Ming scholar Wen Zhenheng writes that plain undecorated boxes should be used, carved and inlaid ones being not sufficiently elegant.

Seal, white nephrite with gray inclusions, ca. 1880, H 2.5 W 2.5 in.

The seal preserves the original pebble shape. Scholars collected seals in many styles engraved with different names and mottos for impressing on letters, paintings, and calligraphies.

The Scholar's Desk

Table screen, white and green jadeite, Qing, late 19th century, H 9.75 W 7.5 in.

The screen created a psychological boundary between the scholar's desk and the outside world, shutting out distractions.

Handscroll, polychrome painting on silk, Qing, late 18th century, H 12.5 W 264.75 in.

The scholar maintained a collection of paintings and calligraphy, mounted with rollers of jade and other precious materials.

Pair of scroll weights, white nephrite with gold gilt painting, Qing, ca. 1850, L 10.5 in.

Brush washer, yellowish-gray nephrite, Qing, 18th-19th century, W 4.62 L 11 in.

The scholar used the brush washer to dip his brush into now and then in order to clean the brush, or to lighten the ink, creating a range of shadings for ink paintings and calligraphy. Free natural shapes, such as peaches or lotus leaves were popular, as typified by this brush washer, in the shape of an upturned lotus leaf.

According to legend, one ancient calligrapher used a pond as his brush washer, the water becoming completely black as he worked at perfecting his style.

Paperweight, celadon nephrite, Qing, Kangxi period [1662-1723], H 1 W 9 in.

Wrist rest, celadon nephrite, Qing, 19th century, L 11 in.

The scholar steadied his wrist on a wrist rest, often made of split bamboo. This wrist rest is formed like a section of bamboo, showing the bamboo joints, and lightly carved with river views and a poem.

Brush pot, dark green nephrite, Qing, early 19th century, H 5.5 W 5.5 in.

Brush, green and white nephrite, Qing dynasty, 18th-19th century,

Brush, yellow-white nephrite, 20th century, L 2.75 W 1 in.

Water dropper, calcinated pale green nephrite, Ming, 16th-17th century, W 5 in.

The water dropper is in the shape of a *Bixie* chimera, a winged lion, one of the oldest mythical animal motifs in world art. The scholar poured water in through the hole in the back, closed with a stopper formed by a small *Qilin* unicorn. From the extended lower jaw forming a coupe, he dripped water onto the inkstone.

Ink sticks, Qing 19th century, H 3.75 W 1.85 in.

Ink (along with paper, brush, and ink stone) is one of "Four Treasures of the Scholar's Studio," The ink sticks, made from a mixture of pine soot and glue, are molded into medallions showing pastoral scenes, with inscribed poems on the reverse.

Ink stone, dark green jadeite, 20th century, L 3.75 W 2.85 in.

The scholar dripped water into the well of the ink stone and ground the ink on the ink stone. The process of grinding the ink was a meditation and a spiritual preparation for the artist. Thus the ink stone is perhaps the most prized of all the scholar's accoutrements.

"Its shape like a broken
  Gui scepter
Its material comparable
  to fine jade
A scholar acquires it
And returns to his true
  self."
  (18th century poet Yuan
   Mei, poem inscribed on
   an ink stone)

Table Screens

Slabs of stone or jade are a slice of nature. Human art was thought to be patterned after nature, and the highest art was described as "stealing [from nature] the process of creation." So the Chinese brought nature into their art by embedding slabs of stone in screens, walls, tables, and chairs.

In the case of marbles the Chinese prized beautiful veins and patterns. In the case of jade, they chose stones with the purest color. On these they carved landscapes and palace scenes, infused with luminous light. A jade screen was a painting in stone.

Pair of table screens, mutton fat nephrite on carved wooden stand, Qing, Qianlong period [1736-1795], H 17.5 W 11 in.

The panels are carved on both sides. On the front are serene scenes of the pleasures of a summer pavilion. On the reverse are peacocks.

PANEL ONE
Three figures in a boat gather lotus blossoms. On the pavilion, one figure holds a fan, and three play a game of *go* as attendants bear a tray of fruit and fan away insects.

Jade table screens were generally carved in pairs. They stood at either side of the father of a household, flanked thrones and couches in the palace, and hid the world from the scholar's table. Groups of four or more panels were set into hinged screens standing on the floor.

"The Lord of Heaven
 summons the Lord
 of Thunder,
To bring his giant axe this
 night and cleave the cliff.
This one slice falls from the
 rocky heights,
Moonlight shining in a cold
 mirror, caught in jade
 casket"

Song on a Purple Stone Screen, by Ouyang Xiu (1007-1072)

PANEL TWO
An oarsman propels a boat through the lotuses, while three figures recline with fan and tea, listening to the flute. On the pavilion shaded by a willow tree, a *qin* lute player accompanies the music while two figures listen.

Four screen panels, green Siberian nephrite, Qing, early 19th century, H 24.5 W 13.5

These panels originally fit into a tall wooden four-panel screen. The panels illustrate court ladies in scenes of the four seasons.

The four seasons are a dominant pattern throughout the art of China, Korea, and Japan. Each season has its tree, its flower, its literary names, and amusements.

SPRING

Two ladies talk on a terrace below a parrot on a perch. They overlook a garden with flowering apricot and willow trees under scudding clouds.

"The sun's warmth melts the ice the world around;
Within the palace gardens, flowers are renewed.
Gentle winds and rain enrich the people;
Rivers and seas are calm; gone is all worldly dust"
  (*Journey to the West*)

SUMMER
One lady plays the Qin lute, while another prepares incense in a tripod, at a flat-topped rock, surrounded by jasmine trees issuing from rockwork.

"The Dipper now points south; the days go slow;
Locust and pomegranate trees contend in brilliance.
Golden orioles and purple swallows sing in the willows,
Their melodious voices drifting through red curtains."
 (*Journey to the West*)

AUTUMN
Two ladies play a game of *go* overlooking a garden lush with chrysanthemums issuing from decorative rocks.

"Fragrant the green mandarin tree; the orange turns to yellow.
Blue pine and cypress welcome frost's coming.
Half-open chrysanthemums make a tapestry on the trellis;
Pipes and songs waft through the watery, cloud-covered land."
(*Journey to the West*)

WINTER
A lady pulls aside the curtain to look at an attendant carrying a lute on a terrace with bamboo, overhung with flowering plum.

"The clouds fly over the rainy sky, all dark and cold;
The north wind blows the snow into thousands of hills.
Deep in the palace the stove glows warm;
They say the plum has blossomed by the jade balustrade"
(*Journey to the West*)

Pair of table screens, green Siberian nephrite, Qing, Qianlong period [1736-1795], H 26 W 19 in.

This pair of screens, of massive size, is a rare example of sealed and datable jade. On the reverse are poems by Peng Yuan-rui; (1731-1803), a poet who rose to the high rank of president of the Board of Civil Office (1789-91).

Peng signs his name in the style of a court official: "Servant Peng Yuan-rui." Given the themes of the paintings, the crane and deer of the immortals, and the fact that the poems were composed by Emperor Qianlong, it is likely that Peng presented these screens to the Emperor in honor of an Imperial birthday while Peng was still in office.

Both scenes are inscribed with a seal of the Summer Palace and a seal reading "Treasure Viewed by the Emperor."

POEM ON REVERSE

The yellow crane flies vast distances
Following the phoenix, it descends from purple mists
It soars up ten thousand miles
The return trip lasting thousands of years.
It rests by the Qing Tian mountain
And often wanders by the gates of a Daoist temple
It is immortal, by nature having a life without end
Its cry resounds throughout the nine heavens.

POEM ON REVERSE

This deer is immortal, a life without limit
Forever it chases after the white clouds
Long has it waited for companions beside the flowers
As it leads the fawns through the bamboo forests

Sometimes it travels to the Jade Stream
Enjoying the smell of golden *Ling-zhi* mushrooms all day
Because it dwells amongst magical cliffs
It has become an immortal and is not aware of it.

Small Pieces

"The superior man of devoted character
Heaps up small things
In order to achieve something great." (*I Ching*)

Small jade artifacts of ages past were favorite collectors items for the scholars. These included sword fittings and archer's thumb rings, as well as belt hooks, pendants, and toggles. Scholars used them as desk ornaments and paperweights, or inset them into wooden boxes and lacquer panels. The Ming connoisseur

Seven thumb rings, nephrite and jadeite, Ming through early Qing, 14th-19th century, H 1 in. (Average) D 1.50 in. (Largest)

Thumb rings originated from the rings used by archers in ancient times. Archery being one of the classical accomplishments of the gentleman, scholars and officials frequently wore thumb rings, a custom lasting until the fall of the Qing dynasty in 1912.

The knuckle-shaped white ring is in the shape of an astragal, a part of the sheep's ankle bone, used for gambling.

Scabbard slide, pale green nephrite, Qing, 19th century, L 3.75 W 1.65 in.

The scabbard slide, another sought-after archaic piece, was the slot through which the sword entered the scabbard.

Sui sword clasp, brown nephrite, Qing, 19th century, L 3.25 W 1.25 in.

The *Sui* clasp was a type of sword fitting. Tied onto the scabbard, it allowed the sword to be swung from the waist. It became a favorite scholar's piece, being much copied in later ages.

Sui sword clasp, gray nephrite, Qing, 19th century, L 3 W .85 in.

Wen Zhenheng suggested that Han belt hooks be attached to the wall for hanging paintings or feather fans.

The Qing dynasty added one completely new object to the jade repertoire: the snuff bottle. Tobacco came into China in the mid-17th century, and by the 18th century the cult of snuff bottles was well established. Fine snuff bottles are still produced today. Perhaps no object in human history has been duplicated in so many materials: glass, crystal, cloisonné, malachite, coral, jasper, marble, etc., and of course, jade.

"Apparently anything was possible," commented George Kates, "except the chance of ever finding a duplicate. This would have been insufferable in Chinese eyes. . . . A Chinese takes special pleasure in using his imagination afresh for such purposes, and fancy's only law, we know, is her inconstancy."

Snuff bottle, white nephrite with green jadeite stopper, Qing, 18th-19th century, H 3.25 W 1.65 in.

Snuff bottle, white nephrite with tourmaline stopper, Qing, 19th century, H 3.5 W 2.25 in.

Snuff bottle, dark mottled green jadeite with tourmaline stopper, Qing, 19th century, H 3.35 W 2.50 in.

Snuff bottle, white nephrite with green jadeite stopper, Qing, 19th century, H 2.5 W 1.85 in.

Snuff bottle, emerald jadeite with black inclusions with rose quartz stopper, Qing, 19th century, H 2 W 1.5 in.

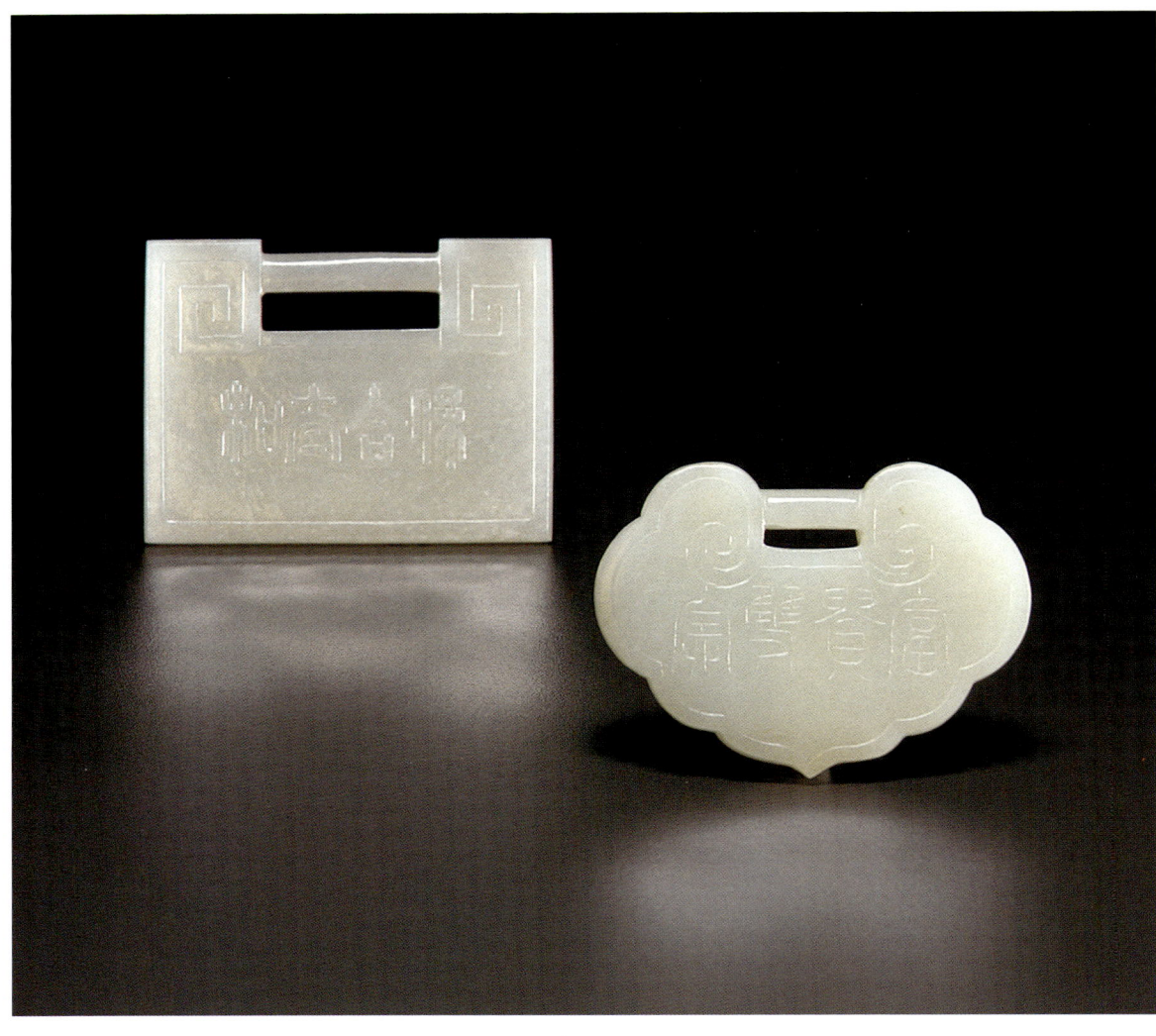

Locket, white nephrite, Qing, 19th century, H 3.25 in.

Lockets, in the form of Chinese locks, were hung around the necks of children to protect against evil spirits. The locket reads "Riches and honor in double measure."

In the famous Qing novel "Dream of the Red Chamber," the hero and the heroine meet and fall in love when they discover that the inscriptions on their lockets match.

Locket, celadon nephrite, Qing, 19th century, H 2 in.

Bi disk pendant, gray and brown nephrite, Ming-Qing, 16th-19th century, H 2.25 W 2.25 in.

Bi disk pendant with Chi dragon, white nephrite, Qing mid-19th century, L 2.75 W 2.25 in.

Bat buckle, brown and green nephrite, Qing, 19th century, L 4 W 2.25 in.

Lotus root pendant, tan and russet nephrite, Qing, 19th century, L 2.50 W 2.25 in.

Bamboo pendant, gray and brown jadeite, Qing, 19th century, H 1.75 W 1 in.

The bamboo shoot, showing the nodes, is a rebus meaning, "To rise, step by step, higher and higher"

Bird pendant, gray and brown nephrite, Qing, 19th century, H .75 W 2.75 in.

The long tail feathers of the bird are a rebus, rhyming with the word *Shou* (immortality).

Turtle toggle, white and brown nephrite, Qing, early 19th century, L 1.75 W 1.35 in.

Oval cabochon, emerald green jadeite, Qing, late 19th century, L 1.75 D 1.25 in.

Of near gem quality, this cabochon would hang as a pendant or fit into a larger piece of jewelry.

The elegant shape of archaic belt buckles made them the most prized of all small pieces. They appear frequently as a design motif, and are thought to have influenced the shape of the *Ruyi* scepter.

Zhuang-zi uses belt buckles as a parable to show how a man achieves excellence by concentrating on one thing. The grand marshal asked his buckle maker what was the secret of his art. The buckle maker replied, "From the time I was twenty I have loved to forge buckles. I never look at other things – if it's not a buckle, I don't bother to examine it."

Zhuang-zi comments: "Using this method of deliberately *not* using other things, he was able over the years to get use out of it."

Belt buckles, nephrite and jadeite, Song through Qing, 11th–19th century, L 5.15 in. (Largest) L 3.25 in. (Smallest)

The buckles include a group of thirty white and celadon nephrite buckles from the Imperial collection.

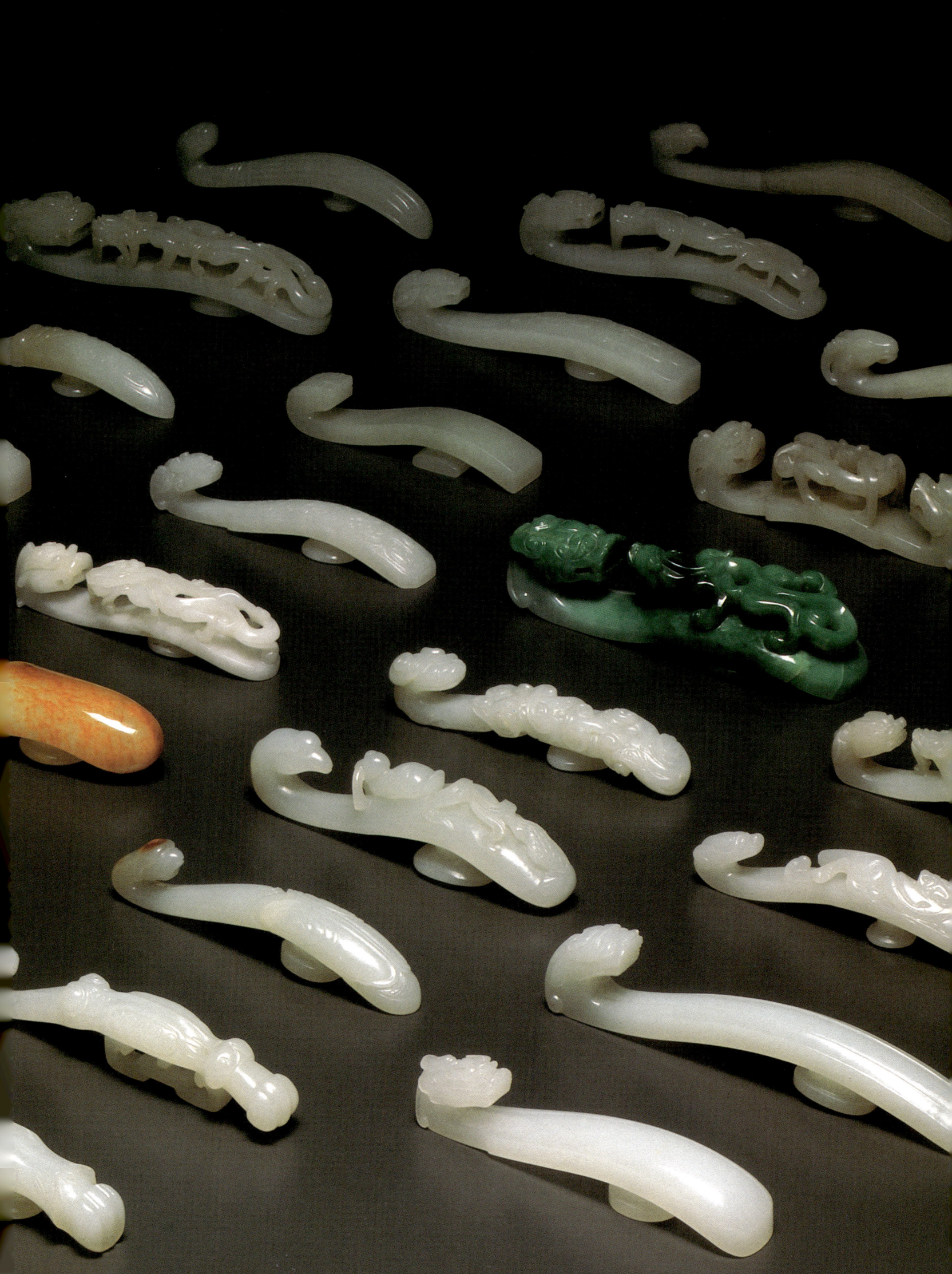

Phurbu dagger, jadeite, coral, and turquoise adorning chased silver, Nepalese, 19th century, H 14.5

Sorcerers used magic triangular daggers, called *Phurbu*, to exorcise the demons of the air. The head of the dagger is the wrathful god *Hayagriva*, who drives away evil influences. The triangular blade symbolizes the three virtues – charity, chastity, and patience, which combat the three vices – hatred, sloth, and lust.

Opposite page:

Chöten Buddhist Reliquary, green and white nephrite, amethyst, turquoise, and ivory, with gilt bronze, Mongolian, Qing, 19th century, H 29.5 in.

A *Chöten* is a Buddhist reliquary, or stupa. It contains a holy relic, such as the ashes of a saint, books, or sacred objects. The typical *Chöten* consists of a round drum, topped by thirteen "umbrellas", rising to the mystic symbol for the sun and the moon.

This *Chöten* contains a seated statue of Avolokitesvara, the Bodhisattva of Compassion (Guanyin), the drum surrounded by eight guardian deities. It stands on a gilt bronze pedestal inlaid with jade panels, coral, and turquoise.

The *Chöten* is a mandala, a cosmic diagram, and every aspect of it is symoblic of occult truths. To build a *Chöten* was to build the body of the Buddha.

Sino-Tibetan Art

Tibet was the home of Buddhist mysticism, remaining until the modern times the "last country where magic still ruled the earth." During the 18th century, the Tibetan cultural region covered a vast area, from the borders of Afghanistan on the west, through the Himalayan states of Nepal, Sikkim, and Bhutan to the south, and across Mongolia and Manchuria to the north.

The Qing emperors, of Manchu descent, patronized Tibetan Buddhism as the religion of the Imperial Court. Tibetan pagodas and temples have left their mark on the city of Beijing, as can be seen even today.

Tibetan sculpture, influenced by India and Central Asia, used jade, turquoise, amethyst and other hardstones as composites, often inset into gilt bronze.

Inset Screens and Panels

The Chinese loved to use one material for another. They made mountains out of ceramics, and flowering branches out of iron.

There was a special fascination with turning stone into painting. In the place of ink painting, marble plaques with interesting veining hung on the wall, looking like views of mountains in the mist. For polychrome painting, the Chinese lapidary used the whole range of hardstones as his palette, while for paper and silk he used jade, marble, wood, and lacquer.

Inlaid panel, celadon nephrite inset with mother-of-pearl and hardstones, Qing, late 19th century, H 12 W 10 in.

The scene depicts the Queen Mother of the West surrounded by Daoist immortals. Materials include: jade, gilding, ivory, soapstone, porphyry, mother-of-pearl, inkstone, jasper, marble, and wood.

Opposite page:

Inlaid table screen, dark green nephrite inlaid with white nephrite and hardstones, on carved wooden stand, Qing, Qianlong period, H 17.75 W 11 in.

The circular screen, one of a pair, shows a *Gu* vase, a *Hu* vase, and a tankard, carved of white nephrite, the latter two with carnelian handles. The three vessels stand on low agate bases. Below them is a tasselled fan in carnelian.

Throne screen, lacquer panels inset with hardstones, with carved wooden auriole and base, Qing, 19th century, H 72.5 W 102 in.

The throne screen stood behind the throne, barring evil influences from the Emperor's back. The lack of a throne screen might mean a "power behind the throne." In 1861, the Empress Dowager staged a coup in the name of her six-year-old son, the Tongzhi emperor, and proceeded to rule China in his name. She sat hidden by silk curtains behind the throne in place of a throne screen.

This screen, composed of five panels, is a cornucopia of auspicious symbols. The aureole at the top consists of jade bats (standing for *Fu*, good fortune) and a jade *Shou* (long life) medallion inset into clouds. The characters, of raised and gilt lacquer, read (right to left): Propriety, Good Fortune, The Crane, Celebration, Long Life. At the top of the central panel is a seal reading, "Calligraphy by the Qianlong Emperor."

The central panel features a vase (green nephrite) with a branch of flowering peonies, symbolic of spring and prosperity, made of nephrite, jadeite, and carnelian. Below are numerous objects suggesting good omens or scholarly taste.

The two panels bordering the center show sun and moon symbols, one incised with peaches, the other with a *Shou* medallion. These rest on clouds (stained ivory) above a group of old pendants (white and celadon nephrite), rising from the backs of mythical beasts (green and gray nephrite).

The outside panels feature hanging baskets of fruit carved of many hardstones: nephrite, jadeite, amethyst, carnelian, coral, etc. suspended from stained ivory stands on the backs of mythical animals.

Chrysanthemum dish, celadon nephrite, Qing, Qianlong period [1736-1795], W 5.25

Moghul Style

"The Hindustan cup is thin as paper, and only the jade worker of that country is capable of making it. The jade worker of the interior acknowledges his inferiority," wrote the Qianlong emperor on a Moghul cup. It was in the middle of his reign that the Qianlong emperor discovered Moghul Indian jades, and he was deeply affected, even shocked.

No matter how finely carved, Chinese jades were "sculptural" and weighty, bound to the earth. Moghul jades on the other hand were delicate, shaped like leaves and flowers, as light as air. Qianlong was so impressed that he brought Muslim jade carvers from Khotan to Beijing and there established a "Western barbarian studio" in 1762.

This profoundly affected Chinese jade artistry. From the later years of Qianlong until the early 20th century, Chinese lapidaries experimented with the so-called "Moghul" style, producing graceful pieces inspired by leaves, tendrils, and flower petals.

Chrysanthemum dish, flecked green nephrite, Qing, Qianlong period [1736–1795]

Not all Moghul style pieces were carved in the Beijing studios. Fine pieces continued to be produced in Western China and in India. This bowl is possibly an Indian piece.

Pair of dishes, green nephrite, Qing, Qianlong period [1736-1795], W 12.25

Opposite page: *Censer*, pale green nephrite inlaid with tourmaline and emerald-green jadeite beads, Qing, early 19th century, W 6 in.

The Chinese artisan is following the Indian taste for inlay with gem stones, such as rubies and emeralds.

Opposite page:
Hu vase, celadon nephrite, Qing, 19th century, H 16 W 9 in.

A tour-de-force of jade carving, very thin, with flower handles supporting two large loose rings, each hollowed out, and pierced. The face depicts palace ladies boating on a lotus pond in the palace.

Hu vase, green nephrite, Qing, 18th-19th century, H 17.75

Typical of Moghul-style pieces, most of the decoration is inspired by flowers. A blossom forms the finial, and vine tendrils support the rings. On each face is an *Apsara*, the heavenly musician of Buddhism. The walls are extremely thin.

The character for jade is three horizontal lines joined by one vertical line through the center, with a dot to the right. The *Shuo Wen* dictionary (ca. 100 AD) says this represents three jades strung together. Thus the character for jade is derived from ancient jewelry.

Hanging pendants, nephrite, jadeite, and metal inlay with metal chain, Qing, late 19th century, H 23.5 W 5.5 in.

The form is archaistic, modelled after ancient girdle pendants. The combination of *Qing* chimes with double fish; is a rebus signifying "Auspicious Happiness in Double Measure."

Jewelry

Jewelry of Shang and Zhou times consisted of strings of jade pendants strung together like mobiles. These hung from the waist and produced a clinking sound as courtiers walked. The Book of Rites (Han dynasty) remarks, "The man of rank . . . hears the harmonious sounds of his jade pendants, and in this way evil and depraved thoughts find no entrance into his mind."

The custom of stringing jades in series persisted until the end of the Qing dynasty. In addition to pendants, jade comprised a multitude of personal adornments, from the beads of mandarin hats, to girdle plaques, to hairpins. Hairpins exist in a vast variety, some carved with great delicacy and originality.

Hanging pendants, white nephrite strung with silk cord, Qing, 19th century, L 28 in.

The central plaque is carved in the shape of a butterfly with antennae developed into peach blossoms. At the top is a *Qing* chime, and at the bottom double fish.

Hairpins, nephrite and jadeite, Ming through Ching, 15th–19th century, L 12.5 in. (largest); L 2.25 in. (smallest)

Modern Jewelry

Modern jewelry is jadeite of gem quality. Appreciation of jadeite as a gemstone began in the late 18th century, the finest jade being used for the mandarin chains of Emperors and officials. Today, pure green jadeite is much sought-after, the best pieces being ranked higher than emeralds and rubies.

Opposite page:
Necklace with pendant, emerald green jadeite, Modern

Ring, emerald green jadeite and diamonds, set in platinum, Modern

Necklace, emerald green jadeite, Qing, Qianlong period [1736-1795]

Very rare, these thirty beads come from a mandarin necklace (originally one hundred and eight beads) said to have belonged to Emperor Qianlong. The beads are hollowed out to shell-like thinness to lighten them and add to the translucence.

Notes

Page	End of noted line	from	Page	Reference
p XI	jade and stone among men		p 6	David, *Chinese Connoisseurship*
p 4	to crush a cubic inch		p 15	Born, *Chinese Jade*
p 5	white in color is the best		p 119	David, *Chinese Connoisseurship*
p 6	black as unmixed lacquer		p 10	*Chinese Jades* (Minneapolis)
p 6	beauty that is unrivalled		p 136	Kates, *The Years That Were Fat*
p 6	as early as 6500 BC		p ii	Huang Xuanpei, *Neolithic Jade*
p 6	gold and silver bars		p 15	*Chinese Jade Throughout the Ages*
p 6	rough stone into jade		p 278-9	Goette, *Jade Lore*
p 6	the jade musical stone		p 217	Ogaeri, *Confucian Memorabilia*
p 6	wanderings of the truth-picker		p 162	Watson, *Chuang Tsu*
p 6	The fairest of stones		p 7	Landman, *Tonkin Collection*
p 8	Heaven is jade		p 142	Goette, *Jade Lore*
p 8	no one has ever seen his form		p 225	Watson, *Chuang Tsu*
p 8	nothing remains unperfected		p 13	Wilhelm, *I Ching*
p 12	requisite of the gentleman		p 5	David, *Chinese Connoisseurship*
p 12	I love the ceremony!		p 169	Ogaeri, *Confucian Memorabilia*
p 14	the side of over-elaboration		p 53	Ogaeri, *Confucian Memorabilia*
p 14	simple fitness of its form		p 93	Wilhelm, *I Ching*
p 15	with heaven and earth		p 8	Shih, *The Literary Mind*
p 15	expressions of the Divine		p 10	Shih, *The Literary Mind*
p 16	cutting away its inborn nature		p 100	Watson, *Chuang Tsu*
p 16	world coalesces into rock		p 38	Hay, *Kernels of Energy*
p 20	palm of the Emperor's hand		p 85	Gump, *Jade, Stone of Heaven*
p 20	right action in human affairs		p vi	Nott, *Chinese Jade*
p 21	flowing into one's hand		p 119	David, *Chinese Connoisseurship*
p 21	beauty of a thousand cliffs		p 38	Hay, *Kernels of Energy*
p 23	long life, many children, etc.		p 115	Cammann, *Chinese Toggles*
p 23	back into them again		p 196	Watson, *Chuang Tsu*
p 25	an imperial seal was death		p 217	Gump, *Jade, Stone of Heaven*
p 28	correct direction in life		Ch 2	Thrasher, *Chinese Music*
p 28	spinning on his hand		p 188	Ogaeri, *Confucian Memorabilia*
p 29	receive the sound		p 175	Goette, *Jade Lore*
p 30	perfumed drum beats		p 213	Frodsham, *Poems of Li Ho*
p 30	Great good fortune		p 196	Wilhelm, *I Ching*
p 36	barks outside the gate		p 256	Wu, *Journey to the West*, Vol I
p 37	monster will lead the way		p 369	Wu, *Journey to the West*, Vol I
p 42	phoenix is seen no more		p 235	Eberhard, *Chinese Symbols*

Page	End of noted line	from	Page	Reference
p 42	magpies fly two by two		p 244	Eberhard, *Chinese Symbols*
p 43	educating his children		p 69	Eberhard, *Chinese Symbols*
p 45	leaps from his nest		p 284	Frodsham, *Poems of Li Ho*
p 46	with numinous radiance		p 251	Wu, *Journey to the West*, Vol II
p 47	imperial dragon too closely		p 6	Cammann, *Some Strange Ming Beasts*
p 48	conquest of the universe		p 12	d'Argence, *Brundage Collection*
p 48	folly brings good fortune		p 23	Wilhelm, *I Ching*
p 50	divine and miraculous		p 136	Wu, *Journey to the West*, Vol I
p 51	years go tumbling by		p 18	Wu, *Journey to the West*, Vol I
p 52	before me that afternoon		p 124	Kates, *The Years That Were Fat*
p 53	resting on his virtue		p 167	Wilhelm, *I Ching*
p 55	down like vast oceans		p 61	Hartmann-Goldsmith, *Chinese Jade*
p 57	jade knives cut the fruit		p 199-206	Goette, *Jade Lore*
p 64	Ping (with a flat base)		p 203	Deydier, *Chinese Bronzes*
p 68	friends come from afar		p 2	Ogaeri, *Confucian Memorabilia*
p 69	'watered' by ancient writings		p 27	Li, *Chinese Scholar's Studio*
p 69	a boat or raft, a palace		p 204	David, *Chinese Connoisseurship*
p 70	not sufficiently elegant		p 192	Li, *Chinese Scholar's Studio*
p 72	at perfecting his style		p 201	David, *Chinese Connoisseurship*
p 73	returns to his true self		p 185	Li, *Chinese Scholar's Studio*
p 74	the process of creation		p 84	Hay, *Kernels of Energy*
p 75	caught in a jade casket		p 86	Hay, *Kernels of Energy*
p 76	gone is all wordly dust		p 507	Wu, *Journey to the West*, Vol III
p 77	drifting through red curtains		p 507	Wu, *Journey to the West*, Vol III
p 78	watery cloud-covered land		p 507	Wu, *Journey to the West*, Vol III
p 79	by the jade balustrade		p 506	Wu, *Journey to the West*, Vol III
p 82	to achieve something great		p 179	Wilhelm, *I Ching*
p 83	paintings or feather fans		p 170	Li, *Chinese Scholar's Studio*
p 83	we know, is her inconstancy		p 46	Kates, *The Years That Were Fat*
p 84	their lockets match		p 65-6	Tsao, *Dream of the Red Chamber*
p 86	to get use out of it		p 245	Watson, *Chuang Tsu*
p 88	magic still ruled the earth		attr.	Guiseppe Tucci
p 88	the body of the Buddha		p 115	Tucci, *Transhimalaya*
p 93	in place of a throne screen		p 64	Weng, *The Palace Museum Peking*
p 94	Emperor on a Moghul cup		p 174	Watt, *Chinese Jades*
p 95	barbarian studio" in 1762		p 41	Hartmann-Goldsmith, *Chinese Jade*
p 101	no entrance into his mind		p 256	Goette, *Jade Lore*

Bibliography

d'Argencé, René-Yvon Lefebvre. *Chinese Jades in the Avery Brundage Collection*. San Francisco: Asian Art Museum of San Francisco, 1977.

Born, Gerald M. *Chinese Jade - An Annotated Bibliography*. Chicago: Celadon Press, 1982.

Cammann, Schuyler. "Some Strange Ming Beasts," in *Oriental Art Magazine*, Vol. II, No. 3, 1956.

Cammann, Schuyler. *Substance and Symbol in Chinese Toggles*. Oxford: Oxford University Press, 1962.

Capon, Edmund, and Macquitty, William. *Princes of Jade*. London: Sphere Books Ltd., 1973.

Catalogue of the Tibetan Collection and Other Lamaist Articles. Newark, New York: Newark Museum, 1950.

Champkins, Paul. *The Minor Arts of China*. London: Spink and Son Ltd., 1983.

Chaves, Jonathan, trans. and ed. *The Columbia Book of Later Chinese Poetry*. New York: Columbia University Press, 1986.

Chen Fu-yen. *Confucian Ceremonial Music in Taiwan with Comparative References to its Sources*. Doctoral Thesis. Middletown, Connecticut: Wesleyan University, August 1975.

Cheng Te-K'un. *Jade Flowers and Floral Patterns in Chinese Decorative Art*. Hong Kong: Chinese University of Hong Kong, 1969.

Chinese Jade Throughout the Ages. Catalogue of exhibition at the Victoria and Albert Museum. London: Oriental Ceramic Society, 1975.

Chinese Jades: *Archaic and Modern, from the Minneapolis Institute of Arts*. Tokyo: Charles E. Tuttle Co., Inc., 1977.

Chu, Arthur and Grace. *The Collector's Book of Jade*. New York: Crown Publishers, Inc., 1978.

David, Sir Percival. *Chinese Connoisseurship, The Ko Ku Yao Lun*. London: Faber and Faber Ltd., 1971.

Deydier, Christian. *Chinese Bronzes*. New York: Rizzoli, 1980.

Eberhard, Wolfram. *A Dictionary of Chinese Symbols*. London: Routledge, 1983.

Frodsham, J.D., trans. *The Poems of Li Ho 791-817*. Oxford: Clarendon Press, 1970.

Goette, John. *Jade Lore*. Shanghai: Kelly and Walsh, Ltd., 1936.

Gordon, Antoinette K. *The Iconography of Tibetan Lamaism*. New York: Columbia University Press, 1939.

Great National Treasures of China, Masterworks in the National Palace Museum. Taipei: National Palace Museum, 1983.

Gump, Richard. *Jade, Stone of Heaven*. Garden City, New York: Doubleday and Co., Inc., 1962.

Hansford, Howard S. *Chinese Jade Carving*. London: Lund Humphries and Co., 1950.

Hartman, Alan, and Poor, Robert J. *Jade as Sculpture*. Catalogue of exhibition at Minnesota Museum of Art. St. Paul, Minnesota: North Central Publishing Co., 1975.

Hartman, Joan M. *Chinese Jade of Five Centuries*. Tokyo: Charles E. Tuttle Co., 1969.

Hartmann-Goldsmith, Joan. *Chinese Jade*. Hong Kong: Oxford University Press, 1986.

Hay, John. *Kernels of Energy, Bones of Earth, The Rock in Chinese Art*. New York: China Institute in America, 1985.

Historical Relics Unearthed in New China. Peking: Foreign Languages Press, 1972.

Huang Xuanpei. "China's Neolithic Jade Ware," in *Ritual and Power: Jades of Ancient China*. Childs-Johnson, Elizabeth, curator. New York, China Institute in America, 1988.

Huang T'ao-peng. *Yuan Ming Yuan*. Hong Kong: Joint Publishing Co., 1985.

Hummel, Arthur W. *Eminent Chinese of the Ch'ing Period*. Washington DC: U.S. Government Printing Office, 1943.

Hyland, Alice R. M. *Deities, Emperors, Ladies, and Literati*. Birmingham, Alabama: Birmingham Museum of Art, 1987.

Illustrated Catalogue of Ancient Jade Artifacts in the National Palace Museum. Taipei: National Palace Museum, 1982.

Ip Yee. *Chinese Jade Carving*. Hong Kong: Hong Kong Museum of Art, 1983.

Jade, A Traditional Chinese Symbol of Nobility of Character. Taipei: China Airlines, 1989.

Joseph, Louis. "Jade in Use," in *Appolo* LXVIII 220-1, Dec. 1958.

Kates, George N. *The Years That Were Fat*. Cambridge, Massachusetts: M.I.T. Press, 1987.

Knechtges, David R., trans. *Wen xuan. Volume One: Rhapsodies on Metropolises and Capitals*. Princeton, New Jersey: Princeton University Press, 1982.

Kuo Pao-chün. *Ku-yü Hsin-chu*. Shanghai: Shen Chou Tu-shu, 1948.

Landman, Hedy B. *Chinese Jade Carvings from the Collection of Dr. and Mrs. Harold L. Tonkin*. Philadelphia: Pennsylvania State University, 1983.

Laufer, Berthold. *Jade, A Study in Chinese Archaeology and Religion*. New York: Dover Publications 1912, Reprint 1974.

Li Chu-tsing, and Watt, C.Y., ed. *The Chinese Scholar's Studio*. New York: Thames and Hudson in association with The Asia Society Galleries, 1987.

Loehr, Max. *Ritual Vessels of Bronze Age China*. New York: Asia Society, 1968.

Lytle, Miriam Anderson. *The Lizzadro Collection*. Chicago: John Racila Associates, Inc., 1982.

Malone, Carroll Brown. *Summer Palaces of the Ch'ing Dynasty*. Chicago: University of Illinois, 1934.

Masterpieces of Chinese Jui Sceptres in the National Palace Museum. Taipei: National Palace Museum, 1974.

Masterpieces of Chinese Seals in the National Palace Museum. Taipei: National Palace Museum, 1974.

Masterpieces of Chinese Tibetan Altar Fittings in the National Palace Museum. Taipei: National Palace Museum, 1971.

Masterworks of Chinese Jade in the National Palace Museum. Taipei: National Palace Museum, 1969.

Na Shih-liang. *Ku-yü Chien-ts'ai*. Taipei: Kuo-t'ai Museum, 1970.

Nott, Stanley Charles. *Chinese Jade Throughout the Ages*. Tokyo: Charles E. Tuttle Co., 1936, Reprint 1962.

Ogaeri Yoshio. ed. and trans. *Confucian Memorabilia*. Tokyo: Hara Shobo, 1964.

Perry, Lillas S. *Chinese Snuff Bottles*. Tokyo: Charles E. Tuttle Company, 1960.

Pope-Hennessy, Dame Una (Birch). *Early Chinese Jades*. London: E. Benn Ltd., 1923.

Reynolds, Valrae. *Tibet: A Lost World*. New York: The American Federation of Arts, 1978.

Salmony, Alfred. *Carved Jade of Ancient China*. London: Han-Shan Tang, 1938.

Schedel, J.J. *The Splendor of Jade*. New York: E.P. Dutton and Co., Inc., 1974.

Shih, Vincent Yu-chung, trans. *The Literary Mind and the Carving of Dragons, by Liu Hsieh*. New York: Columbia University Press, 1959.

Signatures and Seals of Artists, Connoisseurs and Collectors on Painting and Calligraphy Since the Tsin Dynasty. Hong Kong: Arts and Literature Press, 1964.

Strassberg, Richard E., and Foster, Suzanne Haney. *Chinese Jade, The Image From Within*. Pasadena, California: Pacific Asia Museum, 1986.

Thrasher, Alan R. *Foundations of Chinese Music: A Study of Ethics and Aesthetics*. Doctoral Thesis. Middletown, Connecticut: Wesleyan University, 1980.

Tsao Hsueh-chin, trans. *Dream of the Red Chamber*. Garden City, New York: Doubleday and Company, Inc., 1958.

Tucci, Guiseppe. *Transhimalaya*. Delhi: Vikas Publishing House, 1973.

Waley, Arthur, trans. *The Analects of Confucius*. New York: Vantage Books, 1938.

Ward, Fred. "Jade, Stone of Heaven," in *National Geographic*, Vol. 172, No. 3, 1987.

Watson, Burton, trans. *The Columbia Book of Chinese Poetry. From Early Times to the Thirteenth Century*. New York: Columbia University Press, 1984.

Watson, Burton, ed. and trans. *The Complete Works of Chuang Tsu*. New York: Columbia University Press, 1968.

Watt, James C. Y. *Chinese Jades from Han to Ch'ing*. New York: The Asia Society, in association with John Weatherhill, Inc., 1980.

Weng Wan-go, and Yang Boda. *The Palace Museum, Peking*. New York: Harrry N. Abrams, Inc., 1982.

Whitlock, Herbert P., and Ehrmann, Martin. *The Story of Jade*. New York: Sheridan House, 1949.

Wilhelm, Richard, and Baynes, Cary F., trans. *The I Ching*. Princeton, New Jersey: The Princeton University Press, 1st ed. 1950, 3rd ed. 1967.

Wills, Geoffrey. *Jade of the East*. Tokyo: John Weatherhill, Inc., 1972.

Wu Ch'eng-en. *Journey to the West*. Beijing: Foreign Languages Press, 1982.

Wu Yu-chang. *Masterworks of Chinese Porcelain in the National Palace Museum*. Taipei: National Palace Museum, 1969.

Yeung Kin-Fong. *Jade Carving in Chinese Archaeology*. Hong Kong: Chinese University Press, 1987.

Index

Acharya 19
Animals 37
Apsara 7, 48, 98
archaic 2, 6, 7, 8, 10, 12, 26, 31, 61, 64, 82, 86
Archaism 12, 61
astragal 82
Avolokitesvara 88
axes 8, 12
bat 22, 26, 40, 93
Beijing 37, 52, 88, 95
belt buckle 86
belt hook 82
Bi disk VI, 8, 10, 12, 48, 84
Bien Qing 28
bird 15, 36, 37, 67, 85
Bixie chimera 73
Bodhidharma 48
bodhisattva 50, 88
Book of Music 28
Book of Rites 101
boulder XIII, 4, 6, 15, 16, 20
box 21, 31, 61, 67, 70, 82
brush 69, 72, 73
brush pot 68
Brush rest 23, 72
Brush washer 48, 69, 72
Buddha 19, 50, 88
Buddha's hand citron 22
Buddhism 40, 48, 50, 61, 88, 98
Buddhist 26, 48, 50
Buddhist mysticism 88
Buddhist symbols 6
butterfly 4, 23, 44, 100
camel 37
Carved boulder 16, 19
celadon 4, 58
censer 30, 31, 46, 96
Ch'ien Lung XIII
chemical structures 4
Chi dragon 15, 22, 46, 47, 55, 84

chime 6, 28, 29
chimera 44, 45
chrysanthemum 78
Chrysanthemum dish 94
Chöten Buddhist Reliquary 88
color 4, 6, 16, 23, 58, 75
color mixer 61
Confucian Analects 68
Confucian ritual 16
Confucianism 6
Confucius 6, 12, 14, 29, 42, 44
Cong 8, 12
courtly life 2, 52
cutting tool 8, 12
dagger 1, 8, 88
Dao 6, 16, 26, 30, 70
Daoism 6, 8, 16, 51
Daoist 8, 16, 26, 48, 50, 61, 90
deer 44, 80
Ding 30, 34
Ding censer 30
dog 37
Dou 14
Dou vase 14
double fish 100
dragon 6, 10, 12, 13, 15, 20, 22, 23, 29, 31, 42, 46, 47, 54, 67
Dream of the Red Chamber 84
duck 43
elephant 40, 41
Empress Dowager 93
Fang Gu 31
flaming pearl 46
Forbidden City 25, 52
four seasons 76
Four Treasures 69, 73
Fu 22, 26, 40, 93
Fu lion 20, 44, 64
Fu shou 23
Ge Gu Yao Lun 6, 12
George Kates 6, 52, 84

Gu beaker 6, 67
Gu vase 6, 42, 44, 90
Gu Yu Tu Lu 41
Guang 15
Guang libation vessel 15
Guanyin 1, 50, 88
Gui scepter 10, 12, 26, 72
hairpin XIII, 101
Han 8, 10, 12, 37, 41, 82, 101
Hanging Hu Vase 67
hat stand 57
He 21
Heavenly Twins 21
Hehe 21
hibiscus 6, 75
Hindustan 94
horse 23, 37, 41
Hu blade 10, 12, 48
Hu vase 64, 91
Huang Tingjian 69
human figure 48
I Ching 8, 14, 30, 48, 53, 82
immortal 26, 44, 48, 50, 51, 80, 90
immortality 26, 85
Imperial seal XIII, 6, 24, 25, 41, 47
Incense
incense burner 30, 31, 61
incense container 31, 34
Incense Set 31, 34
incense stick 34
Indian 96
ink 73
ink sticks 73
ink stone 73
inkstick 69
Inlaid panel 90
Inscribed pebble 20
Iron 56
Isles of Immortality 51
Jade Age 8

jadeite 4, 5, 6, 13, 23, 29, 34, 40, 42, 43, 44, 56, 58, 59, 66, 69, 71, 82, 84, 86, 88, 93, 96, 101
jewelry 101
Journey to the West 37
Khotan 16, 95
koan 48
Kui dragon 47
Kun Lun mountains 51
Li He 30, 45
ling-zhi mushroom 19, 20, 26, 44, 81
Liu Xie 15
Locket 84
Lohan 19, 51
longevity 61
lotus 43, 61, 67, 72, 76, 98
Lotus root 85
Lung dragon 47
mandala 88
Mang dragon 47
Marriage bowl 52
millet 4, 42, 43
Ming XIII, 6, 12, 14, 15, 20, 36, 37, 41, 43, 46, 48, 54, 55, 70, 73, 82, 84, 101
Moghul 6, 57, 61, 94, 95, 96
Mohs' scale 4
musical stone 6, 28, 67
Muslim 95
mythical animals 58, 93
necklace 103
neolithic jade 6
Neolithic period 8
nephrite IX, 4, 5, 6, 8, 10, 12, 14, 15, 16, 19, 20, 21, 22, 23, 24, 25, 26, 28, 29, 30, 31, 34, 36, 37, 41, 42, 43, 44, 45, 46, 47, 48, 50, 51, 52, 53, 54, 55, 56, 57, 58, 59, 61, 64, 65, 67, 68, 69, 70, 71, 74, 80, 82, 83, 84, 85, 86, 88, 90, 93, 94, 95, 96, 98, 100, 101
Opium pipe 56
paper 69

paperweight 69, 72, 82
peach 22, 61, 72, 100
pebble 20, 21, 70
pebbles 20
pendant 25, 82, 85, 100, 101
Peng Yuan-rui 80
phoenix 42
Plants 22
plaques 25
plum branches 22
pomegranate 22
Qi 22
Qianlong 6
Qianlong Emperor 6
Qilin unicorn 73
qin lute 74
Qing VI, XIII, IX, 4, 6, 13, 14, 16, 19, 28, 29
Qing Chime 28, 29, 100
quail 42
Queen Mother of the West 90
rebus 23, 26, 29, 36, 40, 85, 100
red jade 4
Ring 103
ritual jades 6
ritual objects 12
rooster 43
Ruyi scepter 26, 86
sages XIII, 26, 48, 51
San-shi 31
saws 8
scabbard slide 82
sceptres 25
scholar 69, 70, 71, 72, 73
Scholar's Desk 70
screen panel 76
scroll weight 71
seal 6, 25, 71
seal script 8, 20
Seal Transmitting the State 25
Shang 6, 8, 10, 30, 101

Shou 23, 85, 93
Shuo Wen dictionary 6, 20, 100
Siberian nephrite 5, 63, 76
snuff bottle 82, 83
Song VI, 10, 13, 36, 37, 58, 69, 86
Spider and two crickets on a leaf 4
stupa 88
Sui clasp 82
sword clasp 82
sword fitting 82
Table screen 71, 74, 80
Tang 1, 6, 37, 48
Tao-tie 13, 28, 30, 48, 64
Te Qing 28
Te Qing Chime 28
The Rites 12
Three Abundances 22
throne screen 93
thumb ring 82
Tibet 88
toggle 82, 85
Tongzhi emperor 93
Turtle 85
unicorn 45
Vessels 61
Wan 23
Wandai 23
Water buffalo VI
water dripper
water dropper 73
Wen Zhenheng 70, 82
Western barbarian studio 95
Western China 95
Yang 8, 12, 36
Yi 20
Yin 8, 12
Yuan Mei 73
Yuan Ming Yuan 2, 24, 37
Zhong Bell 28
Zhou 6, 8, 10, 12, 25, 46, 61, 101
Zhuang-zi 6, 8, 16, 23, 86

I said to the almond tree
"Sister, speak to me of God"
And the almond tree blossomed.

(*Photo: Don Madsen*)